Leading with Soul

Humanity's moment in an AI world

MARINA FERNÁNDEZ JULIAN

BALBOA.PRESS
A DIVISION OF HAY HOUSE

Copyright © 2024 Marina Fernández Julian.

All rights reserved. No part of this book may be used or reproduced by any means, graphic, electronic, or mechanical, including photocopying, recording, taping or by any information storage retrieval system without the written permission of the author except in the case of brief quotations embodied in critical articles and reviews.

Balboa Press books may be ordered through booksellers or by contacting:

Balboa Press
A Division of Hay House
1663 Liberty Drive
Bloomington, IN 47403
www.balboapress.co.uk
UK TFN: 0800 0148647 (Toll Free inside the UK)
UK Local: (02) 0369 56325 (+44 20 3695 6325 from outside the UK)

Because of the dynamic nature of the Internet, any web addresses or links contained in this book may have changed since publication and may no longer be valid. The views expressed in this work are solely those of the author and do not necessarily reflect the views of the publisher, and the publisher hereby disclaims any responsibility for them.

The author of this book does not dispense medical advice or prescribe the use of any technique as a form of treatment for physical, emotional, or medical problems without the advice of a physician, either directly or indirectly. The intent of the author is only to offer information of a general nature to help you in your quest for emotional and spiritual well-being. In the event you use any of the information in this book for yourself, which is your constitutional right, the author and the publisher assume no responsibility for your actions.

Any people depicted in stock imagery provided by Getty Images are models, and such images are being used for illustrative purposes only. Certain stock imagery © Getty Images.

Print information available on the last page.

Interior Illustrations: Designed by **Maria Coronado Robles**
Author Photograph: Taken by **Giles Hampton** (*hamptonphotography.co.uk*)

ISBN: 978-1-9822-8945-4 (sc)
ISBN: 978-1-9822-8946-1 (e)

Library of Congress Control Number: 2024925486

Balboa Press rev. date: 12/04/2024

Praise for Leading with Soul

"Marina's books are characterised by a sense of intimacy, a warm and welcoming invitation to pause and reflect. In her second book, *Leading with Soul*, she brings together a collection of interviews, offering the opportunity to learn from a broad range of authentic leaders. These leaders demonstrate that driving success, however you measure it, comes with the soul as much as the intellect. A simple, refreshing, uplifting message—whatever your views on AI might be."

—Jane Jones, Director Partner Enablement at American Express

"Packed with real-world examples, *Leading with Soul* shines a spotlight on leaders who've embraced this soul-led approach and seen their teams thrive because of it. From CEOs to educators, Marina shows how focusing on the human side of leadership, not just the numbers, creates environments where people are motivated, engaged, and inspired. These stories are not just about success in the boardroom, but about leaders transforming lives, nurturing potential, and creating lasting impacts.

The message is clear: leadership isn't just about achieving goals; it's about a deeper connection with the people around you."

—Steve Ball, Founder and CEO, The Process Guru

"Intelligent, witty, and earnest. Marina writes both from experience and the heart. A natural Soul Leader, she offers insights that are both practical and profound. This book is a must-read for anyone curious about self-development, living a more fulfilling, authentic life, and achieving professional growth."

—Julie Parkin, Whole-Health Coach, JP Wellbeing

"We are all born Soul Leaders. Some of us continue our lives building on that gift. For some the truth of who we are gets dulled by academic formulae and business and life pressures. If we were all able to free the truth of what lies within, I am convinced the world would be the kind of place that I wish for my grandchildren - a world that will nourish their talents.

Sadly, that is not currently the case. As I write the news is dominated by the threat of ever new futile wars. If all the science fiction were to come true (and much of it is accurately predicting what will and what is happening as AI becomes more and more sophisticated, we as a human race will become extinct. It is time to say No to the pressures of money, power, and celebrity status. It is time to speak the truth of our hearts and in so doing attract all those who have waited for this lead.

I am fortunate to work with several such people ... and Marina is one of those. This is what gives her the authority to write this book. This is an opportunity to learn how to release the soul power we have within ourselves and shape the world. It is time to take a new direction and here is a book that will support you on that journey."

—Sue Knight, NLP Master Trainer, Author NLP at Work, Coach, and nurturer of future generations.

www.sueknight.com

To Fran,

As you faced a difficult decision, I witnessed you choosing with courage, guided by your heart and soul. In that moment, you brought to life the very essence of what it means to be a Soul Leader. You confirmed what I always have belief: **True leadership is not a position. It's a state of being.**

Thank you for daring to lead with heart and soul.

Contents

Foreword xiii
Preface xvii
The use of this book... xix
Introduction xxvii

Alma's Story: Regaining our Souls 1
Welcome to leading with soul 4
What is the soul 8
Positively Transforming Every Person 16
Unity invites progress 30
Thriving Environments.. 33
Interviewees' Nuggets of Wisdom 37
Education: Shaping Tomorrow's leaders 40
Reclaiming Humanity 54
You Are Highly Advanced 63
Authenticity: The compass of leadership 67
Creative Arts: Society's Truth 70
AI Friend or Foe 87
Insights from Successful Leaders 97
Corporations: Blending heart and strategy............... 101
Coherent Journey 116
Entrepreneurship: Juggling different huts 122
Leaders Connected to a Higher Purpose 138
Charity: Turning pain into purpose.......................... 140
Sports: Building unity through leadership 153

Home: Where everything begins 176
Metaphor for leaders 181
Check lists to assess your current leadership style 186
Humanity's moment in an AI World 190

Final Thoughts 193
Acknowledgements 197
References 199
About the Author 201

Foreword

As an Executive Search Consultant, I meet a lot of senior leaders and naturally end up making decisions on what type of leader they are. So, when Marina asked me to write this it made me think about what makes a strong leader, and how I qualify that.

First impressions are a part of the process, so to balance this I always consider a number of methods when evaluating an individual's suitability for a role, organisation, or team. For example, I will reach out to previous managers, colleagues, and team members to hear their thoughts and learn from their experiences. Combining this feedback with my own assessment will then ultimately form my opinion.

Additionally, the use of psychometric testing and more data driven insight has formed part of this process for decades now. Given the pace of technological advancement, especially AI, the value of this insight has grown exponentially and combined with its easy availability, the process of assessment is more objectively qualified than at any other time.

However, it is amazing to me how often the first impression turns out to being true, so why is that? And how is it that some individuals come across in such a standout way that also inspires others.

In my experience, the traits that characterise strong leaders include their ability to adapt their style to suit whoever they are communicating with, which reinforces the saying that the success of the message is in the receiver. Also, they listen and watch out for body language clues, they are not afraid to acknowledge where others have expertise and experience that outweighs their own, they thrive on bringing everyone with them on a shared journey and take joy from watching people succeed, they surround themselves with diverse individuals who bring differences and diversity of thought to the table and welcome challenge and creativity.

Whether this inspirational quality comes from being an inclusive leader, a leader with strong emotional intelligence, an authentic leader or indeed a 'Soul Leader', I don't know. What I do know is that these types of leaders inspire their teams and businesses every day, whether those businesses are global conglomerates, small family owned firms, sports clubs, or charities. These leaders are not just found in business environments, they are the parents that inspire their children to go the extra mile, the rugby coach that makes a morning in the pouring rain fun for a bunch of kids, the teachers that gently encourage and mould individuals to aspire and dream.

Marina has spent time with a very broad variety of these individuals and this book provides a revealing and thought provoking insight into what it is that makes these individuals stand out from the crowd. It uncovers the essence of being and inspirational, soul-led Leader.

Nina Buttle, Executive Search Partner, Oct 2024

Preface

Dear Reader,

Here I am, sitting in the airport at Toulouse, waiting for my flight to London. With time on my hands, I find myself reflecting on the past few days spent in France.

I was privileged to share some truly special moments with two dear friends, Hannah, and Anna, as we gathered to celebrate Hannah's birthday. Hannah, a leader in her field, has a unique gift for inspiring transformative action, always with a touch of genuine care and attention.

One evening, we were joined by Hannah's friends for a celebratory dinner. As we raised our glasses, each person at the table took a turn to speak. Their heartfelt reflections left us in awe. They spoke of Hannah's ability to touch lives through her soulful leadership, a quality that has clearly impacted many.

It was clear that the people around the table were what I call Soul Leaders. These individuals lead from a deep place within, from their very souls. Their words were unfiltered, free of pretence and titles, resonating with raw, genuine truth.

Their words reminded me of the incredible impact people can have on one another and the powerful connections we forge when we engage at a deeper level.

In that moment, I thought about you, dear reader. Pause to consider the extraordinary qualities you possess as a human being: your creativity, which sparks innovation; your imagination, which transforms dreams into reality; and your intuition, which guides you with clarity. You have free will and every decision you make, no matter how small, shapes the course of your life and the lives of those around you. And let's not forget your capacity to love, to feel, and to empathize. Emotions carry you through moments of joy, sorrow, and everything in between; It is through these experiences that we truly come alive.

These qualities are what make us unique.

Yet, as the world accelerates and artificial intelligence reshapes our lives, we risk losing touch with these very traits. In the pages that follow, this book will challenge you to reconnect with what makes you human. It's an invitation to lead with the soul, connecting your inner wisdom to thrive in a world dominated by technology.

Whatever you do, you are leaving a mark on this world. Are you having the impact you truly wish to have?

With gratitude,
Marina

The Use of This Book

Is This Book for You?

As we embark on the pages that follow, take a moment to reflect on whether these questions align with your goals and challenges:

- Have you ever thought about leading in a way that just feels right for you?
- Are you dreaming of being a leader who makes a positive difference?
- Are you eager to create a meaningful impact in your household, community, or workplace?
- Are you wondering what kind of leader at home or at work you are or want to become?
- Are you already leading with soul and want to explore some exercises?
- Are you ready to embrace a fresh perspective on leadership?

Consider this book your compass for navigating the ever-changing landscape of decision-making reinforcing the unique leader in you. It's your guide to thriving in humanity's moment in an AI world.

Is This Book Not for You?

This book may not resonate with everyone. Here are some considerations that might indicate this book isn't the perfect fit:

- You might not care for this book's message if you are not comfortable with leading with soul.
- Individuals who imitate the behaviours of artificial intelligence rather than engaging in authentic human interactions might not be the right readers.
- People devoid of emotions may find this book less resonant.
- Those lacking a desire for growth might not find this book to their liking.

What Is This Book All About?

This book invites you to explore and perhaps transform how we approach life and one another. It calls us to enrich our human connections and embrace a revitalised form of guidance that is both expansive and inclusive.

In today's world, relying solely on our minds and bodies is no longer enough. It's time we join forces with another form of intelligence, our souls.

By uniting our knowledge, intellect, and inner wisdom, we can keep pace with the rapid changes of life. Our greatest strength lies in deepening our connections with the most profound parts of ourselves and one another.

I believe we have the potential to harness the synergy between artificial and human intelligence. Leading with soul enables us to tap into this synergy, empowering us to thrive in humanity's moment in an AI world.

What's in This Book for You?

Are you ready to transform how you lead and make decisions in every area of your life? If so, you're in the right place. In these pages, you'll learn to harmonise intelligence, knowledge, and inner wisdom as the driving force behind your actions.

At this pivotal moment in history, as AI reshapes our world, this book serves as your compass. It invites you to lead with your most authentic human qualities, enabling you to make a lasting and genuine impact.

In the dance between humanity and technology, it's our essence that must take the lead. Humans and AI are not competitors; one is alive, the other is not. As the world evolves, so too must we, especially in how we guide and inspire others. Creativity, empathy, and connection will always be our defining strengths.

This book goes beyond theory. It shares real-life stories of soul-led leaders who have faced challenges and emerged stronger by leading with inclusivity and coherence. You'll explore the type of leader you are or aspire to become while uncovering why nurturing human connections is vital for flourishing in all areas of life.

What's more, this book acts as a mirror, offering insights into your leadership style and personal strengths. With this self-awareness, you'll amplify your impact not just at work, but in your home, your relationships, and your community.

This isn't a book about AI. It's a conversation about how people flourish, and communities thrive when human-led efforts take centre stage. Above all, it's a reminder that our experiences, relationships, and contributions are uniquely human and meant to be shared.

At its heart, this book invites you to embrace your humanity and shift how you lead. Unlike AI, which is powered by algorithms, your essence is rooted in lived experiences, deep connections, and qualities that amplify not just your actions, but the impact you leave behind.

Exercises: The Creative Experiences in This Book

Explore the practical 'Creative Experiences' in this book designed to help you pause, reflect, and connect with your inner wisdom. These exercises will guide you in integrating your inner leader into your daily life and stay on track.

Stories from Soul-Led Leaders

For some time now, I've noticed a particular type of leader, one who inspires people in a profoundly different way. These leaders stand apart, displaying traits that resonate deeply with those they guide. Intrigued by what makes them so unique, I set out to explore what distinguishes their approach and how they create meaningful connections.

In shaping this book, I sought to uncover how leading with soul can profoundly influence individuals, organisations, and society as a whole. Through engaging conversations and research, I discovered remarkable journeys across diverse fields, each story painting a vivid picture of the impact and effect we have when we lead with our souls.

A Broad Spectrum of Influence

Education stood out prominently. Leaders in this space are shaping our future by guiding our children in becoming evolved leaders. The creative arts provided another lens, addressing sensitive topics like disability and other social issues creating a positive community change. In the business world, entrepreneurs and digital creators are rewriting possibilities, embracing innovation while keeping people at the heart of their efforts.

Charities, by focusing on those with hidden challenges, demonstrated how compassion and purpose can resonate universally. Sports brought communities together, challenging mindsets and promoting unity. And then there's the cornerstone of it all, family. In families, where our foundational values are formed, leading with soul has more than a positive impact, it becomes the engine for harmony, validation, and growth for everyone involved.

A Common Thread

When I merged these stories from education, the arts, business, charity, sports, and family life, a clear and powerful picture emerged: leading with soul is universally relevant.

It transcends professional boundaries, personal circumstances, and societal roles. These leaders' stories and insights are shining examples of inclusive leadership, positive influence, and the harmonisation of their environments. Their impacts ripple through their professional achievements, family dynamics, and personal well-being. They remind us that the world needs more leaders who lead with their souls; people who lead with humanity, heart, and commitment across all aspects of life.

An Invitation

I hope the stories shared in this book, regardless of the context they come from, inspire you. Whether you're guiding a team, nurturing a family, or simply striving to leave the world a little better than you found it. Let these examples serve as a reminder: leading with soul transforms everything it touches.

INTRODUCTION

We are living in a world where artificial intelligence (AI) is rapidly reshaping every aspect of our lives, from workplaces to homes, technology is evolving faster than we can comprehend.

And with it comes a pressing question: how do we stay connected to what makes us human?

For too long, we've relied on intellect alone to guide us, leading with our minds, detached from our hearts. The consequences of this approach are plain to see rising mental health challenges, an epidemic of disconnection, and a collective hunger for authenticity and meaning.

At the same time, we're glued to screens, caught in an endless loop of emails, apps, and alerts, surrendering our autonomy to the very technologies we created to serve us.

And just as we're facing these challenges, AI has arrived as both an opportunity and a test. For some, it feels like a threat; for others, it promises revolutionary change. But no matter how you view it, one thing is clear: It's time to give birth to a new way of living and leading, one that is coherent with who we are, grounded in our humanity.

It's humanity's moment to lead with soul while embracing technology.

Machines can process data, but they cannot feel or love. They cannot bring depth or meaning to life. That's our domain, and it's time we reclaim our passion for life.

This book is about what can happen when leading with our souls in an era defined by algorithms. It's an invitation to embrace inner wisdom, creativity, and connection while navigating the challenges and opportunities presented by AI.

Leading with Soul isn't just for CEOs or managers. It's for parents, educators, professionals, and anyone craving deeper human connection.

In these pages, you'll find insights, real-world stories, and practical exercises to help you lead with authenticity and courage, no matter your role in life.

Let's explore what it means to Lead with Soul and seize this defining moment together.

Alma's Story: Regaining our Souls

In my tranquil office, scented with citrus and bathed in warm light, Alma sat across from me, her shoulders heavy with the weight of her struggles. Her weary eyes spoke of exhaustion and disappointment, the marks of someone who had been carrying too much for too long.

Alma had reached out to me after reading my book, Balance. Its message had struck a deep chord within her, revealing how her soul had slowly been slipping away.

She worked in an environment where success was measured solely by metrics, and where AI systems were valued more than the people who operated them.

As she settled into the chair, her voice trembled, filled with vulnerability. In the safety of my office, the walls she had built to protect herself from her relentless professional environment began to crumble.

She described endless hours of work, decisions made without regard for their human impact, and a workplace culture that viewed people as tools for profit rather than individuals with value.

"It's all about the numbers," she said, her voice breaking. **"There's no kindness, no meaning. It's like humanity has been replaced by automation."**

Alma wasn't just losing her passion for work; she was losing herself. As a brilliant and dedicated leader, she had once been full of purpose and spark. But the relentless pursuit of corporate success had worn her down. She felt as though she had to leave her soul behind every time she walked into the office, and eventually, she stopped picking it up on her way home.

Her identity, her strength, and her essence had faded, leaving behind a shadow of the person she once was.

One evening, after yet another soul-draining day at the office, Alma found herself at the train station. The bright light in her eyes had been replaced with emptiness, and she was struck by a chilling thought: **"I understand why some people give up and throw themselves onto the tracks."**

That moment became a turning point. Alma realised she had to reclaim her soul. She couldn't continue sacrificing her identity and purpose at the altar of corporate efficiency.

Her journey sparked something profound within me.

As I reflected on her story, I was struck by the immense weight carried by so many in work cultures that neglect the humanity of their employees. It's not just individuals who suffer, this invisible burden moves through families, communities, and society as a whole.

We are witnessing a quiet tragedy; one that unfolds in our workplaces, homes, sports teams, and schools.

And it must stop.

Alma's courage to confront her reality planted the seed for this book. Her story became a reason for me to act, urging me to deeply explore the essence of leading with our souls, not just as a coach o trainer, but as a believer and advocate of humanity.

For every Alma out there, forced to choose between their soul and their job title, sacrificing their love for life in pursuit of external success, this book is for you.

It's time to realign our values, nurture our souls, and reclaim our identities.

Together, let's rediscover ourselves and reignite our passion for life and work.

WELCOME TO LEADING WITH SOUL

In a world where logic and reason often rule, and behaviours are becoming increasingly transactional, leading with soul offers a breath of fresh air. It's not just a philosophy; it's a way of making decisions that honour the wisdom of our human qualities alongside our intellect. Leading with Soul explores what can happen when lead using our human innate qualities, placing emphasis on shared values, genuine connections, empathy, and a sincere care for the well-being of those we guide.

Leading with the soul transcends job titles. It's not confined to roles or personalities but rather focuses on the ability to ignite greatness within others. True advancement isn't about individual success, it's achieved when every person within a group thrives and flourishes.

Why Now is the Time to Embrace a New Model of Leadership

As emotions seem to fade and mental health concerns reach alarming levels, leading with the soul has become a necessity. It's no longer just about self-preservation, it's vital for our relationships, careers, businesses, and communities.

Picture a future where humans are either obsessed with or fearful of AI and robotics. The meaningful connections that define our humanity decrease, leaving us more disconnected and isolated. Mental health deteriorates even further, eroding the fabric of society. Humans thrive on touch, warmth, and connection, qualities machines can never replicate.

Yes, AI is brilliant, efficient, and even life changing. But no matter how advanced it becomes; it lacks an inner life. Only another human can truly feel what you feel. The more we integrate AI into our lives, the more critical leading with our souls becomes.

Leading with soul is a human-centred approach.

It's a natural and congruent way of leading that adapts to each individual and prioritises what makes us uniquely human: our emotions, intuition, and creativity. In addition to our empathy, resilience, and ability to form meaningful connections.

Think of it as a harmonious integration of everything we are.

It's not about shunning technology but rather incorporating it in balance with our human essence, creating a richer, more inspiring way of living and leading. This way of guiding ensures that we stay grounded, ethical, and connected to what truly matters.

Leadership Is Everywhere

Guidance isn't reserved for CEOs or high-ranking officials. It manifests in daily interactions that impact others, no matter your title. We are leaders in our homes, workplaces, schools, clubs, and communities.

For too long, we've been taught that success comes from leading with our heads while ignoring our hearts. This way of thinking has brought power to the few but misery to the many.

True leadership isn't about dictating from a pedestal; it's about inspiring and guiding others towards a shared vision. It's about walking alongside them, nurturing trust, and collaboration. Leaders that lead with their souls prioritise human connection, using empathy and integrity to make decisions that benefit everyone not just themselves or their companies.

Ask yourself: Are we still clinging to outdated ideas of leadership; Are we guiding others in ways that match the needs of today's world? Can we lead in ways that honour who we truly are while igniting greatness in others? I believe we can.

We can free ourselves from conventional views of leadership as a distant, hierarchical role. Instead, imagine leaders as partners walking alongside their teams, engaging in dialogue, and collaborating on shared goals. This shift creates relationships built on trust, respect, and shared humanity.

This is what it means to be a Soul Leader, a leader for a new era. Why Now? Because We Don't Just Want to Survive. We Want to Thrive.

What is the Soul

Have you ever felt your heart swell as you watched a sunset, or experienced a connection with someone so profound it left you breathless? That, perhaps, is the soul stirring within you. But what, truly, is the soul?

This question has captivated and puzzled humanity for centuries. Yet the essence of the soul often eludes precise definition. Trying to define the soul is like trying to catch sunlight in your hands; it's there, you feel its warmth, but it always slips through your fingers. It's that indescribable feeling when you hold a newborn baby for the first time or when a melody moves you to tears.

The soul, in its countless interpretations, is often regarded as the very essence of an individual. It's the invisible core of who we are, representing our innermost being. I like to think of it as an unseen thread that weaves our emotions, thoughts, and experiences into something greater, something beyond what the mind alone can comprehend. It's what makes us truly human, a field of intelligence that transcends mere physical existence.

The soul is intangible, eternal, and essential and everyone has one. It's the part of ourselves that stretches beyond the physical body, connecting us to something larger than our individual existence. This connection between mind, body, and soul shapes how we see ourselves, our relationships, and our place in the world. It's the "you" that cannot be seen but can always be felt; like a whispered secret hanging in the air, words unspoken but deeply understood.

When we speak of the soul, we are tapping into our capacity for connection, emotion, creativity, and moral depth; qualities that distinguish us from every other form of life. The soul is not something we can fully explain; it is what remains when words fall short. It's the breath we take in the stillness of the night, the quiet observer within that reminds us we are alive.

And perhaps this is the soul's greatest gift: its mystery. A mystery that defies rational explanation yet invites us to feel, to wonder, and to embrace the unknown.

> **Your soul is the most intimate part of you, and it isn't found by running away.**
> **—Deepak Chopra**

Why haven't we connected with our souls sooner?

Why haven't we connected with our souls sooner, embracing it as a natural way to lead? I believe there are three main reasons: modern lifestyle, religion, and education.

The concept of the soul isn't new. Throughout history, humanity has dipped its toes into its vast ocean but has only scratched the surface, hesitant to go deeper, afraid of the unknown.

Truly exploring our inner selves, understanding our mission, and leading consciously can feel daunting, even eerie, like venturing into a dark cave with no idea what lies ahead. And let's be honest: we humans love control. We cling to the comfort of what we can see and manage, reluctant to surrender to the uncertainty of introspection.

But fear of the unknown is only part of the problem. While religions and cultures have woven intricate beliefs around the soul, modern life presents an entirely different challenge: an obsession with external success that leaves little room for self-reflection.

It's remarkably simple when you think about it. Instead of seeking answers outside ourselves, we need to realise our wholeness and turn inward to use all the parts we're built with. Yet, our fast-paced world conditions us to focus outward. We are directed, like sleepwalkers, to chase status, achievement, and productivity, so we barely notice the parts of ourselves quietly crushing from neglect.

Even so, I sense we are turning a page. We are stepping into an era that demands the renewal of behaviors, fresh perspectives and expansive ways of approaching life and business. More than ever, we'll need to draw on the wisdom of what makes us human; our values, emotions, and connections to thrive in this rapidly changing world. **It's no longer a question of whether connecting with our souls is important; it's essential.** If we don't, we risk losing touch with the very essence of who we are.

Our Modern lifestyle

A Personal realisation. I'll admit, I didn't always walk the talk. For a while I parked my essence thinking my lack of touch with my soul wasn't going to catch up with me. I was mistaken.

For a long time, I was one of those people who believed that doing more was the key to serving others and living a meaningful life. My days were a blur of constant activity, driven by the notion that productivity equals value. The harder I worked, the more disconnected I felt from myself, from others, from life itself. Something was missing. And as painful as it was to admit, I realised that "something" missing was my essence, my soul.

Realising this wasn't easy. For the longest time, I thought pushing through exhaustion and distractions would eventually lead to fulfilment, but it didn't. I reached a point where I could no longer ignore the truth: doing more wasn't helping me or the people I cared about. I was running on empty, caught in a cycle that left no room for reflection, growth, or connection.

That's when I decided to take a step back and turn my focus inward. It wasn't a decision I made lightly, and it wasn't easy. At first, sitting with myself, just sitting, felt deeply uncomfortable. I started with meditation, but even that felt alien to me, like I was fighting against the very wiring of my brain. My instinct was always to move, to fix, to solve. But something told me to persist. And so, I did. Bit by bit, I began to reconnect with something I thought I'd lost in adulthood: that quiet, invisible part of me I hadn't paid attention to in years. To my surprise, it was still there, waiting patiently. It hadn't disappeared, as I'd feared. I learned that we never truly lose this part of ourselves, it's always available to us, no matter how long it's been neglected.

The Turning Point. This new perspective changed my life. It reminded me that no matter how disconnected we feel, it's never too late to turn inward and find ourselves again. It's not always easy, and it takes courage to face what we've ignored. But the rewards are immeasurable. For me, this journey wasn't just about finding peace, it was about reclaiming the invisible parts of me. And in doing so, I've been able to serve and connect with others far more authentically than I ever could while simply "doing more."

This personal journey is proof of what I now believe wholeheartedly: we don't need to wait for the "right time" to reconnect with our souls. The right time is always now.

Our Growing Disconnection

Over time, I've watched human connection deteriorate at all levels. Loneliness is rising. Depression is more pervasive than ever before. We're forgetting who we are and what we need to grow and thrive, and it's taking an enormous toll on us.

As technology evolves, streamlining our decision-making and even our creativity, there's a growing risk that humanity will lose touch with its values, emotions, and beliefs. The early signs of this disconnection are already here. And with AI playing a greater role in shaping our lives, the need for embracing new behaviors has never been more urgent.

Our Education

Education, a foundational force in shaping our worldview, is perhaps the most glaring missed opportunity. For most of us, school taught us to solve math problems, memorise historical dates, and recite scientific formulas, but it failed to teach us something just as critical: how to connect with ourselves. We've been given no tools to explore the essential aspects of who we are or what we need to thrive as human beings. How can we be expected to nurture our souls when no one has even explained why it matters?

Imagine if education shifted to include this. What if schools taught children to explore their emotions, values, and purpose? What if we raised a generation that valued human interconnectedness as much as it valued academic success?

Perhaps this is the missing piece that could guide us toward a future where AI is developed and used ethically, complementing humanity instead of diminishing it. But the truth is, we're not machines. And that's why connecting with our souls is so vital. It's not just about finding peace or meaning; it's about reclaiming our humanity in a world that's increasingly losing touch with its core. This is not a luxury to explore when we "have time." It's a necessity, one we can no longer afford to ignore.

I believe now is the perfect time in history to set aside our fears, doubts, and judgments. Let's face it: those things rarely grow anything fertile. Instead, let's focus on reclaiming ourselves, individually and collectively, united under the banner of humanity for the betterment of all.

Who knows what wonders we might uncover when we fully embrace the wisdom of the human soul? What if empathy and compassion are just the beginning? What if reconnecting with ourselves opens doors to entirely new dimensions of possibility, dimensions we can't even imagine yet? One thing is certain: we won't find out until we try.

So, let's begin, together.

> **Neglect of our spiritual well-being has left many of us experiencing a "sick soul": weariness of heart, existential dread, and a sinking feeling that nothing really matters—without finding a way out.**
> **—Deepak Chopra**

Positively Transforming
Every Person

In the many roles we play, as a parent shaping the future, a CEO steering a company's course, a headmaster guiding young minds, or anyone standing at the forefront of something, the shift from traditional leadership to leading with soul is no longer optional; it's essential.

Why? Because it transforms positions of authority into meaningful responsibilities, infusing every interaction with depth, meaning, and purpose. It's also the most natural and sustainable way of guiding and inspiring others.

Think about it: while conventional leadership provides structure, Leading with Soul adds depth, connection, and meaning not just to tasks, but to the essence of those you lead. For a parent, this means understanding your child's dreams and fears, and guiding them with wisdom that goes beyond rules. For a team leader, it's about creating a workplace where individuals thrive not only professionally, but personally. For a headmaster shaping young minds, it's not about transactional knowledge transfer, we are not machines. It's about igniting a love for learning.

Whether you're in the bustling kitchen of a household, in the therapy room, or even in the boardroom, this model of leading enables both individual and collective success. Soul-led leaders know their roles extend beyond strategy and decision-making. They remain deeply attuned to the needs, aspirations, and unique qualities of those they guide.

These leaders transform everyone they interact with. They adapt their messages to their audience, cultivating relationships that inspire and uplift.

I've witnessed the transformative power of soul-led leadership in homes, organisations, and businesses. Now, as the world craves genuine connection, purpose, and well-being, leading with our souls isn't just important; it's essential.

Wherever you find yourself in the classroom, on the football pitch, in the music hall, or in the heart of a bustling company, lead in a way that positively transforms those you interact with. Reflect for a moment: how many lives can be enriched when you lead from this deep, soulful field of intelligence?

In preparing to write this book, I explored countless research papers, articles, and thought pieces. Many themes emerged, and the reflections of Chief Rabbi Jonathan Sacks particularly resonated with me.

In his seminal work Morality, Sacks highlights the pressing need for a shift from a society rooted in individualism to one that celebrates collectivism. He advocates for a more synergistic society, where the ethical compass is aligned with the collective "we" rather than the singular "I."

Sacks champions the common good, urging us to transition from an "I-centred" mindset to a "we-centred" tapestry of shared values and goals. His reflections underscore the importance of generosity, collaboration, and unity in creating a future that is not only more equitable but also more prosperous.

Dr Zareen Roohi Ahmed echoes these sentiments in her book The Gift, drawing upon Sacks's wisdom. She reminds us that while the business landscape often glorifies competition, true progress comes when we embrace collaboration and generosity. These values promise a future enriched by equity and collective prosperity.

It's time to move beyond individualism and embrace a collective mindset. Let's create a society built on unity, collaboration, and generosity. And let's not overlook that beautiful word: generosity.

> **People who need people are the luckiest people of all.**
> **—Barbra Streisand**

Who Is a Soul Leader?

Picture a leader driven by something deeper than just goals or objectives. Someone who is deeply connected, self-aware, and attuned to the people they lead. This is a Soul Leader.

Soul Leaders see empathy, authenticity, and compassion as strengths, not as traits to be hidden. They invest time in understanding their people, not just their roles. For them, leading others is not merely about hitting targets; it's about aligning with core values and putting others first.

These leaders are catalysts for change and create positive outcomes in organisations, communities, and beyond. They build meaningful relationships, cultivate excellence, and adapt their messages to resonate with diverse audiences. They embrace vulnerability as a strength and lead with unwavering commitment to the collective good. Grounded in their values, they inspire and propel success, leaving an impact that goes far beyond surface-level achievements.

Examples of Soul Leaders

Take Jane, a CEO who leads with her soul. Jane isn't simply chasing profit margins; she dedicates herself to understanding the personal struggles and dreams of her team. On more than one occasion, she has quietly covered the cost of a critical operation for an employee who couldn't afford it, showing that her people aren't just numbers. They're valued members of the company family.

Jane knows that leadership begins with the environment she cultivates, so she listens. Employees have a voice in how the company operates, and she acts on their feedback. For Jane, leadership is about achieving goals while nurturing the growth and well-being of her people. The result? A fiercely loyal team, driven to excel because they feel genuinely cared for.

Now consider Mother Teresa, an iconic human who devoted her life to serving the poorest of the poor. Her leadership wasn't about authority or control; it was deeply rooted in empathy, compassion, and an unshakeable understanding of human suffering. Even today, her legacy continues to inspire millions to lead with kindness, purpose, and heart.

Leaders like Jane and Mother Teresa aren't confined to boardrooms or global missions. They exist in our homes, schools, and everyday lives. Once you've crossed paths with a Soul Leader, you never forget. Their impact is unforgettable, leaving an imprint that lasts a lifetime.

Some may call these leaders inclusive, conscious, or purpose driven. I call them Soul Leaders. Why? Because at its core, the soul embodies all these qualities and more. It's the essence of who we are, and what transforms everything.

How does a leader become conscious? By tuning into their humanity and aligning with their inner self. Jenna Faye Madden, CEO of Soul Meets Strategy and New Earth Leadership, describes conscious leaders as those who lead transparently, operate from their hearts, and remain committed to personal growth. These leaders tune into themselves, their missions, and their communities, using their influence as a tool for personal, spiritual, and professional development.

Michelle Obama beautifully captures the essence of conscious leadership:

"True leadership, leadership that lifts families, sustains communities, and transforms nations, rarely starts in palaces or parliaments. True leadership is not just about dramatic events that change history in an

instant. Instead, it often begins with the smallest acts, in the most unexpected places, by the most unlikely individuals."

Foresight, perseverance, and the ability to inspire, are what distinguish great leaders. They empower others, communicate with integrity, and guide groups towards shared visions.

Today, we stand at a pivotal moment in history as AI weaves itself into the fabric of our lives. Successfully integrating this technology requires far more than technical expertise. It demands a deep understanding of human emotions, relationships, and connections.

As AI reshapes how we live and lead, those in guiding roles must strengthen their own and others awareness. Technology should enhance our humanity, not replace it. The responsibility falls on us to ensure AI enriches, rather than diminishes, what makes us truly human.

Satya Nadella, CEO of Microsoft, perfectly sums up this sentiment: "AI cannot replace human qualities like creativity, empathy, and judgment. Instead, AI will amplify our human capabilities and help cultivate our creative spirit."

As leaders, it's time to embrace this blend of humanity and technology to lead consciously, authentically, and with soul.

Who Can Lead with Their Soul?

As I delved deeper into this research, a series of questions came to mind: Is soul-led leadership a privilege reserved for a select few or an open choice available to everyone? Does it belong only to top executives, or can anyone embody this transformative approach? Is it rare, or is it more common than we think?

These questions led me to explore the inclusivity and accessibility of leading with soul across all aspects of life.

Is Soul-Led Leadership Reserved Only for Big Organisations?

Absolutely not. You don't need a corner office or a fancy title to lead with soul. Leading with soul is for everyone, everywhere. Whether you're a parent creating a loving home, a CEO running a multinational company, or an individual managing the daily chaos of life, you can lead with your soul.

Leading with Soul isn't limited to boardrooms or corporations. It's a powerful principle that resonates across all aspects of life. It aligns with what truly matters to us as humans and brings that alignment into how we guide others. Imagine this way of leading as a compass, one that uplifts others and creates a positive difference in their lives.

Leading with Soul isn't just a leadership style. It's a way of being. A model like this, focused in achieving results as much as it does in creating a deeper connection with the people around us, allows people the freedom to be themselves. This way of being transcends size and setting; it speaks directly to the heart recognising the humanity in yourself and those around you.

What set these leaders apart?

You might wonder, what exactly sets these leaders apart? They aren't defined by degrees, titles, or rankings. What truly distinguishes them is how they lead, with vulnerability, care, and a deep understanding of others.

Those who lead with their souls are hands-on, leading by example inspiring others through their actions. **Whether formally educated or not, they share one thing in common: high emotional intelligence and an extraordinary awareness of their own emotions and the needs of others.** They are attuned to the human qualities that drive transformative change.

Soul-led leaders uplift and celebrate others. They are the heartbeat of the places they lead; the silent observers who notice everything.

They invest time in truly understanding the people around them: their joys, their struggles, and their dreams.

At the core, it all boils down to one thing: genuine care. They bring love and dedication to their work, nurturing excellence not just in themselves but in those they lead.

These qualities set them apart, putting them at the forefront of positive change. And here's the thing, their influence doesn't come from their position at the top of a hierarchy. It's rooted in the inspiration they evoke in others. When people witness the way they lead with integrity, compassion, and a relentless pursuit of excellence, they can't help but be drawn in.

A Reminder of What Matters Most

Here's the truth: what truly matters isn't a fancy title or lofty position. It's what you choose to do, how you do it, and the positive impact you have. Whether or not you consider yourself a leader, being human in all its messiness, beauty, and depth is the most effortless way to inspire others to be their best.

When you lead with soul, you care deeply and bring an internal passion to your actions, enhancing personal satisfaction, strengthening relationships, and creating a positive impact on the lives of those around you.

Whether navigating the complexities of family dynamics or guiding a large organisation through turbulent times, leading with soul, places humanity at the centre, aligning your essence with the collective good and forging bonds that resonate with everyone you touch.

If you want to be this kind of leader, the path is simple yet profound: cultivate these values every single day and watch how it transform every relationship and interaction you have.

The Shared Qualities of Leaders

All great leaders, whether conventional or soul-led, possess qualities that set them apart: resilience, vision, and a drive for growth. They treat challenges as opportunities, viewing setbacks as stepping stones to return stronger and wiser. These leaders are guided by a clear vision, recognising potential where others see obstacles.

While conventional leaders may focus on structure and strategy, soul-led leaders prioritise emotional intelligence and empathy. Yet, both approaches are meant to create environments where progress flourishes, and learning becomes a natural part of daily life.

Great leaders inspire their teams to push beyond limits and encourage a culture of continuous improvement. Their positive influence leaves a legacy, shaping not only the success of the company or community but also the personal development of those they lead.

Whether you identify as a conventional leader, a soul-led leader, or somewhere in between, remember: these qualities are within reach. Embrace them and transform the way you lead, making a lasting impact.

Nature or Nurture?

You might wonder whether this way of leading is something you're born with or if it can be learned. There is truth in both, as you will read later. For some, it's a natural inclination, part of who they are from the start. For others, it's a skill that develops over time, shaped by their experiences and the world around them.

Whether innate or developed, it's a journey of growth and transformation sparked by becoming attuned to the needs of those around you. A common thread binds them together, a deep commitment to integrity, care for others, empathy, and purpose. As one of the leaders I interviewed put it:

> **One of the things that sets Soul Leaders apart is that they care; they really, really care. It is genuine, it is authentic, it matters to them personally, not just professionally.**
> **—Dominic Mott, Headmaster of Hurstpierpoint College**

What Soul Leaders Value

As the book progresses, a question that I hope to solve for you is, what are the values of those who lead with their souls?

They hold integrity, honesty, and congruence in high regard. They value their own well-being as well as that of those around them. They treasure time, and they approach life with a receptive mindset. They believe in reciprocity, giving and receiving. They know all too well the price they pay when they don't respect these principles and the significance it holds for themselves and those under their guidance. Striking a balance between action and rest is key.

Leading with the soul requires going deep into one's innermost self-examining values and boundaries, accepting one's humanity beyond individual desires.

These leaders are clear in why they are doing what they are doing. They are doing it because we are interconnected. They know that what they do impacts every individual within their sphere, and they remain firm in their commitment to serving others, even in the face of discomfort and sacrifice.

They carry the weight of their decisions with a keen awareness of the change they can make not just today but in the future. For this reason, they continuously reassess their beliefs, letting go of what no longer serves them or their team.

Taking care of themselves isn't always instinctive for these leaders. Sometimes, it takes experiencing burnout to learn the importance of looking after every part of oneself: mind, body, and soul. Self-care means making time for oneself, reflecting on one's thoughts and feelings, and adding fun and playful activities, as well as moments of peace, into one's life. It is something these leaders learn to value.

They place their attention in finding happiness, staying active, and setting clear limits for themselves and others. Being active helps them be less stressed and more effective leaders. All these habits improve their well-being and enable them to genuinely bounce back from challenges with strength.

Those who lead with their souls are committed to continuously working towards inner excellence and personal development.

They practise openness, flexibility, and vulnerability and maintain a curious mindset. Acutely aware of how their actions impact others, they ask for feedback ensuring everyone is on the same page and aligned towards a common goal. However, they understand the necessity of making tough decisions and taking ownership of the outcomes.

Unity invites progress

Take the example of Martin, the owner of a tech company. Martin believes honesty and transparency are key to growth and evolution. He encourages his employees to take ownership of projects, step outside the company's comfort zone, and make decisions autonomously. Empathy, care, and compassion drive Martin's leadership. He values diverse perspectives, even when they challenge his own. For Martin, others' viewpoints are not just tolerated; they are actively sought and deeply respected.

During the COVID-19 pandemic, Martin's company faced unprecedented challenges and was on the brink of closure. He could have focused solely on logistics and budgets. He could have made redundancies to protect the company's bottom line. But Martin chose a different path.

Grounded in his true self and unafraid of vulnerability, Martin called a company-wide meeting. He spoke openly about the struggles the business was facing, admitted mistakes he had made, and shared his sleepless nights worrying about the impact of potential layoffs on employees and their families.

He reminded his team of the importance of staying united in such a challenging time and went a step further by offering his personal resources to support employees and their loved ones. His honesty and humanity sparked something extraordinary.

The team followed Martin's example. Employees offered their own resources, skills, and time to help one another through the crisis. Relationships deepened, and individuals who had barely spoken before began supporting one another as if they had been lifelong friends. They weathered the storm together, learning invaluable lessons about the power of staying together in one direction, and resilience.

Years later, following a highly successful campaign, Martin took time to thank his team, praising their collective effort and the bonds they had built. He attributed the company's survival and thriving future to the unity and strength they had cultivated during those difficult times.

Martin's approach to leadership extends beyond the workplace. His dedication to his team's well-being resonates in their homes, families, and broader communities. It's not surprising that his employees are passionate, dedicated, and willing to go above and beyond. When we lead with our souls, we create legacies that inspire far beyond our immediate reach.

Martin's story reminds us of the profound impact we have. When leaders of any kind put their people at the center, they create places where individuals and communities thrive. The result? High morale, increased productivity, and a shared sense of purpose.

And Martin's story is just one of many. The pandemic revealed countless examples of human connection, community resilience, and the extraordinary things we can achieve when we prioritise each other. These moments remind us of what we're capable of when we ditch narrow, individualistic thinking in favour of a more expansive, collective mindset.

Guiding with soul nurtures relationships that endure far beyond the length of a contract or the life of a campaign. It drives meaningful progress that touches lives in ways spreadsheets and statistics never can. Its impact is felt in families, communities, and generations.

At the core of Leading with Soul is a simple truth: we need depth and human energy to thrive.

THRIVING ENVIRONMENTS

Too often, leaders fall short of creating environments where individuals can truly thrive.

Leading solely with the mind is no longer sufficient to navigate the complexities of our modern lives. It's like having a navigation system with no internet connection, it won't take us where we want to go. Before knowing it, we're lost, frustrated, and unable to deliver. Worse still, the passengers coming along for the ride, our teams, families, or communities lose trust in us.

Despite having more resources and conveniences than ever, something vital seems to be missing when it comes to building thriving environments. What could it be?

We're not leading from our inner intelligence.

The intellect, while powerful, lacks the capacity to deliver everything we need on its own. We've become disconnected from our humanity, forgetting that our soul, the essence of who we are, can guide us far better than the intellect ever could.

Whether you're a parent on a school patio, a friend longing for meaningful connection, or a leader striving to inspire transformation, you may already sense the limitations of leading solely with the mind. The missing link lies in leading with the soul; an approach that goes beyond managing tasks and people, diving into the heart of human connection and purpose.

What Thriving Looks Like

Imagine a household where decisions resonate with each family member's unique needs not just strategic decisions, but ones that nurture understanding and care. Picture a community where bonds are built on empathy and shared values, not just surface-level interactions. Envision a company where leaders truly listen, developing environments where creativity and collaboration thrive.

These are the environments where people feel alive; where they are supported to grow, innovate, and contribute meaningfully. They encourage autonomy, self-responsibility, and cooperation, becoming places where individuals feel empowered to do their best. What if we built more of these spaces? What if, instead of focusing solely on outcomes, we began with the simple human need for connection?

By leading from our inner wisdom, we can:

- Create workplaces that celebrate diverse perspectives and invite bold ideas.
- Encourage emotional intelligence and creativity in every setting.
- Teach children to rely on themselves while understanding their shared impact on the world.

Children, after all, are tomorrow's leaders. When we infuse empathy, compassion, and care for community into their education, we set the stage for future workplaces and homes where respect, unity and collaboration are the norm. They'll grow up knowing that **leadership is about connection and communication, not control** and that's a powerful lesson.

The leader of the future

When I think about the leader of the future, I imagine someone luminous. A person who skillfully laces together human connection, technology, and inclusivity. Just envision it: workplaces where colleagues function as

Leading with Soul

communities, homes where families share not just spaces but genuine moments, and communities where everyone feels seen and heard.

This image makes me smile.

We can create environments where people thrive and feel inspired to do their best. Leading with Soul taps into the wellspring of the human qualities that lies within each of us. Adopting this way of leading and being, transforms duties into meaningful actions and teams into thriving unified communities.

Together, we can create spaces that uplift everyone, cultivate excellence, and honour the humanity in us all.

Interviewees' Nuggets of Wisdom

- Leaders who lead with their souls care; they really, really care, and not just professionally but personally.
- If leaders do not find a balance, they may save their businesses but lose their souls.
- There is no leader without a team. A leader must be well to lead, and the company culture must be embodied by the company's members for resonance and harmony to occur.
- Leaders hold a profound responsibility to be true to themselves.
- A genuine leader not only inspires but empowers others to become leaders themselves.
- The real beauty of leadership lies in watching people thrive and lending a hand to their success.
- Soul Leaders are testaments to the resilience of the human spirit, the glue for communal resurgence.
- It is the individual who matters.
- Leadership is not just about the company; it's about the people in it.
- If you're not genuinely loving what you're doing and finding purpose in it, your work and your leadership of others will reflect that.

- Taking responsibility seriously, with compassion, is what sets apart a true leader.
- We are expressions of divine love.
- Only a heart knows what another heart longs for.
- Joy is found in shared experiences and happiness with our teams and families.
- Fulfilment isn't a single euphoric moment; it's an ongoing journey found not in the achievements but in the shared experiences and genuine happiness of teams and families.
- Bringing your soul into conversations helps others to open and be vulnerable.
- Self-care isn't a luxury; it's a lifeline.
- We wear so many different hats; if we don't take time for self-care, we run the risk of developing multiple personality disorder.
- It is possible for a business to be a vehicle for compassion and positive change in the world.
- We are here not just to feel love but also to do love.
- If you are intent to do something that affects others, you need to connect with the ripple effect that this action will have in the world.
- Everything is a consequence of your effort and mentality.
- We can't control what happens to us, only how we respond.

- The impact you leave on others is determined by how you make them feel.
- A healed human being is much more beautiful than a human being who never suffered.
- The success of the message is in the receiver.
- Whatever you do, you are leaving a mark in the world. Are you having the effect you wish to have?

Education: Shaping Tomorrow's Leaders

I firmly believe that education lies at the heart of our growth and development. It is within the walls of our schools that we begin to shape who we become.

A child's academic success, well-being, and overall happiness often reflect the leadership approach of their school. A school that prioritises personal growth and connection over mere academic achievement sees this priority mirrored in its students, the school environment, the teachers, and, by default, the home.

Many of us have witnessed the damaging effects of unskilled or emotionally disconnected teachers on students. Conversely, we've also experienced the transformative power of educators who focus on stimulating learning experiences and genuine conversations with their students. These exceptional teachers spark curiosity and ignite a lifelong love for learning.

I'll always remember the profound impact one of my teachers had on me and how her words forever changed the course of my life. When I was thirteen, she shared something that struck me deeply: I could choose my own values rather than simply absorbing those of others. She told me I had the qualities of someone who leads with soul and that my greatest responsibility was to stay true to who I am.

This teacher celebrated differences in others without exclusion and consistently ignited greatness in those she guided. She didn't just teach; she inspired. Her self-assurance and authenticity left an indelible mark on me. Not everyone celebrated her boldness, but her influence on me remains unforgettable.

Today, I understand that we find people most inspirational when their approach resonates with our own learning style.

Yes, our educators hold immense power over what we believe is possible and how we perceive ourselves. For me, that single conversation planted a seed that has continued to grow ever since.

 **Talking with Dominic**

I recently had the privilege of speaking with Dominic Mott, Headmaster at Hurstpierpoint College, whose approach exemplifies my deep admiration for soul-led leadership. Together, we explored the profound impact of Leading with Soul in education, touching on topics such as qualifications, vulnerability, and the importance of humour in cultivating relationships.

We also discussed the role of human essence and values in guiding the leaders of tomorrow. Our conversation extended to building resilience, prioritising well-being, and unlocking potential. Critical areas that shape not only students but the educators who influence them. What follows is an extract from our discussion.

Embracing Humans: A Renewal in Leadership

When it comes to hiring teachers, their qualifications matter, but what counts most are their potential and their human qualities. I seek individuals who possess a sense of purpose, meaning, and creativity; individuals who offer something unique. I believe in teachers who are driven by their hearts and can create magic that inspires students beyond the curriculum.

I highly value educators who can connect with children on their level, those who are enthusiastic and foster curiosity and creativity. These teachers and leaders encourage students to share their fresh ideas, and experiment with new concepts and take risks, creating an environment where learning is exciting and rewarding.

By staying true to who they are, teachers open doors to new possibilities, empowering students to thrive.

Vulnerability and Meaningful Conversations

Identifying the person behind the job title is essential in creating an environment where mistakes are perceived as opportunities for growth. Accepting each other's humanity, including flaws, allows for relaxation that enables genuine conversations.

To promote this way of connecting, it's essential to set aside authority and approach conversations as equals, signalling a willingness to listen and learn together. This shift leads to better and deeper interactions and more receptive and coachable teachers. This approach allows me, as a leader, to understand teachers' needs and concerns and have meaningful conversations that end in the growth of all involved.

Embracing Our Journey to Avoid the Pitfalls of Conventional Leadership

When engaging with leaders in other schools that adhere to a more traditional approach, we must embrace our journey and consider potential traps and pitfalls when borrowing ideas. We should use them as opportunities to innovate and develop creative solutions tailored to our unique challenges.

At our school, we prioritise creating an environment that encourages internal problem solving. We believe that young teachers have a wealth of innate resources and skills that they can tap into, and in doing so, they strengthen their capabilities, inviting collaboration and camaraderie among colleagues. As a result, they stretch their imaginations, build stronger relationships, and cultivate a sense of community and belonging within the school. This approach ultimately leads to school and individual success as well as fulfilment for everyone.

Cultivating Growth in Our School Community through Soul-Led Leadership

Emphasizing potential and adding training and feedback shape the development of future leaders; nurturing this model and culture creates a unique climate for leadership and an environment of constant growth.

We invest in our teachers, coaching them to their fullest potential and promoting them based on their capabilities. Through our internal leadership programme, we facilitate the growth of medium-level leaders into senior positions, creating a pipeline of future leaders who benefit our school, our broader community, and humanity. Coaching is the cornerstone of our staff training, ensuring those in our school community have the support and resources needed to thrive.

Empowering Our Children for Life Beyond the Classroom

Our leadership programme makes sure that not only do the teachers have the knowledge to deliver the curriculum, but they also have the tools to coach students so they can identify what their own needs are. It goes beyond the teachers to the children to inspire them to solve their problems and trust that they have resilience. This innovative model enables students to take control, stay in touch with their emotions, and prepare not just for school but for life beyond school, rather than relying on a leader to tell them what to do.

We have a system were students coach other students. We have set up a family in each of the boarding houses we have so students' emotional needs are covered, having family support when they are not only at home but also at school.

By using this coaching model rather than following direct instructions, children leave the school confident in their skills, prepared for the wider world, and ready to lead the complexities of life outside the school. This approach aims to enable the thinkers and leaders of the future, humans connected to their emotions who put their hearts and souls into whatever they do, leaving a mark in this world.

Placing Students at the Heart of Our School

At the core of our school's mission is a steadfast commitment to prioritising the well-being and growth of every individual student. Our fundamental purpose is not merely to serve the institution but to ensure the holistic development of each pupil, regardless of their abilities.

This ethos shapes every aspect of our culture and decision-making processes. By embracing this higher purpose, we strive to create an uplifting environment where every student can thrive and reach their full potential. This commitment to student-centredness is not just a guiding principle; it's the very soul of our school.

Understanding Our Role in Every Moment to Navigate Different Situations with Intention

For a school leader, each moment presents a unique opportunity to make an impact. Whether walking into the school chapel or preparing for an event, I am aware of what is expected and required of me. Recognising the importance of clarity and unity in providing a message to the community in different spaces helps me navigate different situations with intention. However, it's in the one-on-one interactions that I have the opportunity to connect with individuals. These moments allow me to understand their needs, concerns, and aspirations on another level and help me cultivate genuine connections that build trust within the community.

Connection Through Humour

In my journey towards leadership, I've discovered the importance of balance between seriousness and levity. One of my mantras is, "I take what I do seriously, but I don't take myself seriously." Humour can be used as a constant reminder to approach my role with dedication and passion while also being open to moments of humour and lightness.

Humour, when used appropriately, serves as a connector that can be very powerful. It allows me the space to establish rapport and forge connections with others. While my job holds significant importance to me, incorporating humour into the right situations can break down barriers and create a sense of camaraderie among colleagues and team members.

Leading with Soul to Understand and Connect with Our Audience

As a headmaster, it's crucial for me to remember that the individuals I lead are young people. If I can't embody that infectious, childlike sense of wonder, I won't be able to connect with them effectively, and perhaps I might even be in the wrong profession.

My role isn't just imparting knowledge; it's also influencing and inspiring students to want to learn.

These interactions are reciprocal; they influence me just as much. I constantly consider who is shaping my role as a leader, primarily the vibrant young minds around me. Adapting my message and being responsive to my audience and learning from them is just as essential as leading them. This dynamic exchange rejuvenates me and instils a deep joy and passion for learning.

 **Soul-Leading Story: Demonstrating Commitment in Difficult Times**

The following describes a moment at the school that helped me understand the broader role of leaders within a school community.

When the lockdown came, there was a need to provide continuity of education. And most schools managed this to some extent. At our school, our remit was much broader, as it was not just the academic education we were thinking of, it was the fully rounded educational experience that we knew our pupils thrived on.

This need meant putting our sports provision online, running activities such as Combined Cadet training via

Microsoft Teams, getting the choir to record songs via Web Link, keeping the full schedule of assemblies and chapel services, and generally trying to keep the school running as smoothly as possible, not for the sake of it but because this is the form of rounded education, we believe in. Our transition into teaching online needed to be the online education we aimed to offer.

Second, we recognised this was a tough time for parents as much as the children. So, we needed to reassure them and make it as easy as possible for them to navigate their way through lockdown and the impact on their work. Keeping their children well engaged was part of our way of helping struggling parents manage their way through the pandemic.

Third, we needed to be more than just an employer. We needed to give stability and reassurance, such as making a clear commitment that we would not be laying anyone off during the pandemic, and regularly thanking those staff who were on furlough for playing their part in keeping the business model afloat.

The pay cut that the leadership team agreed to take voluntarily was also part of a show of solidarity with people's livelihoods. But more than that, we also needed to give a sense of community and purpose. Regular communication through video clips helped keep a sort of connection that was so important. Reaching out to do check-ins with our staff on an individual basis gave them a sense that they were valued, and they are.

All the above is an oversimplification of the realisation that our pupils, parents, and staff needed us as, and that they needed strong and compassionate leadership.

We were able to see the positive impact such direction can have on people's lives. And this helped to crystallize our role as leaders who care about not just the organisation we run, but the people the school exist to serve.

Advice for Future School Leaders

As you embark on your journey as a leader, it's essential to define your educational philosophy and identify what you believe to be most important.

Every decision you make, every structure you create, and every aspect of your organisation's culture should align with this philosophy.

Stay true to your beliefs and principles and resist the temptation to chase metrics or conform to external pressures. Instead, focus on creating an environment that reflects your educational values and promotes the holistic development of your students.

By staying true to your educational philosophy, you will inspire others, creating lasting positive change in your community.

Soul-Leading Thoughts

In conventional leadership, it's easy to get caught up in a mindset of prioritising what's best for yourself or your company. However, Leading with the soul challenges this notion.

When guided by your soul, you may find yourself making decisions that go against conventional wisdom. For instance, if you believe someone would thrive elsewhere, you must trust your intuition and prioritise their needs over those of your organisation; even if it means creating a gap that needs to be filled again.

Ultimately, leading with your soul requires a willingness to listen to your inner voice and act with integrity, even when it's difficult or goes against the status quo. By embracing this approach, you have access to a more authentic and compassionate leadership style, one that benefits individuals and organisations alike.

A Creative Experience: for a Clear Mind

Our minds are like office spaces, often cluttered with endless to-do lists, unresolved thoughts, and distractions. This mental chaos can leave us feeling overwhelmed and less productive. What if you could organise your mind, like tidying up your workspace, to create a clearer, calmer headspace?

Take a moment to imagine your mind as an office. Close your eyes and step inside. How does it look? Is it neat and functional, or are there piles of papers and chaos everywhere? This is your space, so take a deep breath and begin to change it.

Sort and Shelve Your Thoughts

Visualize gathering your thoughts and concerns, sorting them into neat boxes. Label each box with a subject, perhaps "work," "family," or "dreams." Then place these boxes on an imaginary shelf. Keep going until nothing is left scattered in your mental space.

Look around: is there anything still lying around? Maybe a forgotten piece of paper or an overdue task. Tidy up every corner until the office is pristine.

Add Light and Inspiration

Now, picture a large window opening in your mental office. Let in a soft, warm light, like the gentle glow of a winter sun. Feel the light illuminate your space, giving it life and clarity. Imagine placing a small plant on your desk as a symbol of growth, and add a note of encouragement; something simple, like "You've got this!" or "One thing at a time."

Close the Door with Gratitude

As you finish, step back towards the door of your imaginary office. Before leaving, take a moment to look around and feel gratitude for your mind. Thank it for working so hard, even when it's cluttered or overwhelmed. Then gently close the door behind you, leaving your mental space tidy and at peace.

Check In with Your Mind

How does your mind feel now? Can you sense the difference? Embrace this feeling of clarity and emptiness. Commit to returning to this space whenever you need to declutter and refocus. With this refreshed mindset, approach your tasks one at a time, following a priority that feels right for you.

Reclaiming Humanity

As I prepared to attend a networking meeting in my hometown, I took a moment to read the provided bio and strapline. The words "a chance to make more meaningful connections" caught my attention. It got me thinking: What makes connections truly meaningful? Why are they so important? This curiosity led me to explore how technology and AI might impact the authenticity of human relationships.

While technological advancements undeniably bring gains in efficiency and productivity, I found myself contemplating a potential trade-off. Could the use of AI overshadow the joy and depth derived from meaningful human relationships?

Consider the place where you work today; perhaps it's a bustling office where colleagues collaborate sparking spontaneous moments of creativity. Picture the daily dramas, the shared laughter during breaks; a universal language that transcends job titles and hierarchy.

As you navigate your tasks, you engage in lively conversations, exchanging ideas and offering insights that contribute to the collective creativity of the team.

Now, let's fast-forward to a more automated workplace where the focus is about efficiency. Everything functions flawlessly and on time, but the vibrancy, creativity, and spontaneous joy of personal interactions have faded. The invaluable moments that brought energy, emotion, and soul to your workdays have become increasingly scarce.

The heart of the workplace is replaced by sterile, transactional digital exchanges.

How long do you think you could work in such an environment without it affecting your productivity, emotional well-being, and creativity?

Don't be a downer, Marina. We can turn this around; I tell myself while I explore it from a different perspective: Personal face to face interactions brings value and energy to our work; integrating them with AI can create a win-win situation for everyone involved.

While AI brings efficiency, human connections and expressions of emotions ensures a holistic and resilient work environment. A space that harmoniously blends the irreplaceable human touch which nurtures, with innovation, adaptability, and a positive culture is a thriving place.

> **People are craving depth and human-to-human connection now more than ever, meaning the expectation is rising for authenticity, vulnerability, and relationship-based interactions.**
> **—Jenna Faye Madden, CEO of Soul Meets Strategy and New Earth Leadership**

A World Without Connection

Imagine a world where our rich and deep interactions with others are severed. Well, you don't have to imagine it; just remember. Revisit the early days of the COVID-19 pandemic when isolation became the norm. Initially, some of us may have welcomed the solitude as a temporary social break, a bit like a bliss bubble. But as time passed, the energy we derived from face-to-face exchanges began to fade.

Fast-forward to today. Envision a scenario where traditional interactions are replaced by efficient yet emotionally sterile interactions, with AI taking the place of human warmth in meetings. How would this feel? What would be the consequences?

The advantages of such a scenario are clear, precision, efficacy, and convenience. But the aftermath could be a profound human crisis. Isolation would lead to loneliness, deteriorating mental health, and a collective struggle against disconnection.

Take the case of Alex. At nine years old, during a crucial period of emotional development, she was abruptly cut off from her friends. Isolated in front of a computer, she began muting or deleting her peers whenever conflicts arose. When Alex returned to school, her headmaster expressed concerns about her lack of social skills and emotional intelligence.

Today, Alex still struggles to connect with others, feeling unseen and unheard. She's starting to believe she has no emotions.

This isn't just Alex's struggle. The COVID era revealed how disconnection can impact people of all ages, including leaders who face impostor syndrome and low confidence. After all, we are what we repeatedly do.

What Are Meaningful Connections?

Meaningful connections are the treasures we discover in life's adventures. They're the genuine relationships that bring depth and joy to our days.

Imagine, or recall from your memory, that you're at a bustling networking event, surrounded by a whirl of faces and conversations. Amidst the hustle, you start a conversation with someone who shares your passions. What begins as small talk quickly turns into an engaging exchange of ideas, dreams, and shared values.

As you talk, you notice there are many commonalities between you, and you're both eager to explore more about each other. Before you know it, a spark of creativity ignites, and you find yourselves collaborating. You've made a link, a bond that goes beyond the surface, a relation driven by shared aspirations and mutual respect.

In the months that follow, this connection blossoms into a friendship. You stand by each other, offering support, celebrating victories, and lending a listening ear during tough times.

This friendship becomes more than just uplifting energy, it evolves into a source of inspiration and companionship, reminding you that life is more fulfilling when shared with others. It's a prime example of a meaningful connection, one that adds depth and purpose to life's journey.

Meaningful interactions are deep, honest relationships that infuse our lives with trust and support. They extend beyond surface-level interactions and involve genuine exchanges of emotions, energy, thoughts, and motivations. They're defined by mutual respect and shared values.

Why Do We Need Connection?

If you've ever wondered why we crave meaningful relationships, picture this: amidst life's challenges, two individuals form a bond that becomes a lifeline, offering emotional support during tough times.

You share stories that create a unique bond, alleviating each other's pain and motivating each other to do your best. You see yourself reflected in the other.

Simply put, people need people.

Meaningful connections provide us with a sense of belonging and acceptance as part of a valued community or network. Unlike the sterile codes and algorithms of AI, they offer renewed energy and joy; a safe harbour where we can rest and rejuvenate.

These relationships are catalysts for personal growth, offering diverse perspectives and insights through shared experiences. Positive and meaningful relationships also enhance our overall happiness and life satisfaction, adding emotional richness as we share joy, achievements, and even challenges.

Beyond emotional benefits, having reliable people to turn to during difficult times reduces stress and acts as a buffer against life's challenges.

We all want to be seen, to be heard, and to know we're not alone. Strong social interactions with others are linked to better physical and mental health, resulting in lower stress levels, improved immune function, and increased longevity. Want to stay healthy and young? You know what to do: invest in your connections!

> **Life can be confusing and painful. Sometimes we just need to be with one another in that confusion and pain, saying, "I see you. I hear you. I'm with you." In that presence, there is love. And perhaps at the root of it all, that's what we need most.**
>
> **—Cory Muscara**

The language of the heart

Daily conversations over tea, sharing stories of joy and struggle, and exploring the nuances of human emotions, all these contribute to the richness of our lives.

While AI will one day exhibit highly advanced capabilities, it will never replicate the emotional depth and unique essence of human experience. Meetings where meaningful connections blossom is indispensable to our well-being.

We have a responsibility to care for those we guide. Let's create spaces that encourage genuine, face-to-face interactions. After all, the language we humans best understand is the language of the heart.

So don't wait. Go outside. Make friends. Laugh. Take risks. Get burned. Cry. Wipe your tears and start over. Because numbness is not a pretty place to live.

> **If you talk to a man in a language he understands, that goes to his head. If you talk to him in his own language, that goes to his heart.**
> —**Nelson Mandela**

A Creative Experience: Reimagining Relationships

Take a moment to imagine a world without phones, computers, or any form of digital technology. In this world, how would you engage and link with the people around you? What kinds of conversations would you have with your family and friends? What activities would fill your days?

Close your eyes and fully immerse yourself in this imagined world. Picture the faces of those around you, how do they look? Are they smiling, laughing, or perhaps struggling? Notice how this imagined world makes you feel.

Now, consider the world you live in today. What would you miss from the present digitalised world if it were gone? And, more importantly, what benefits might emerge in a world grounded in deeper, undistracted human connection?

Take your time with this reflection. As you envision this alternate reality, think about how these insights might influence the way you connect with others in your life now.

You Are Highly Advanced

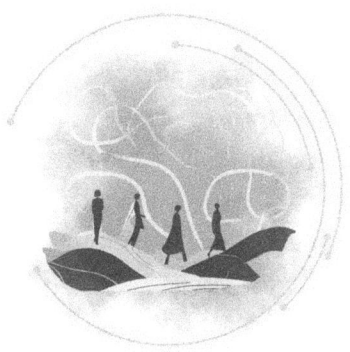

We humans are highly advanced, sophisticated beings. In fact, no other species creates what we can, and that's what makes us unique. Think of a musician composing a symphony, a perfect blend of creativity, emotion, and technical mastery. This kind of expression is distinctly human, showcasing the unparalleled depth of our capabilities.

We think with autonomy, make our own choices, and solve problems without external input. Our intelligence is vast, encompassing intuition, creativity, emotional depth, and interpersonal skills. These qualities enhance our awareness and compassion, enriching not only our own lives but the lives of those around us. This intelligence, however, doesn't originate solely from the mind, it comes from something deeper, what we might call the soul.

Staying connected to this source, alongside the mind's brilliance, is what keeps us whole.

We are also incredibly adaptive beings. Our ability to evolve is one of our greatest strengths, perhaps this is why we've embraced technology so eagerly. AI may complement our natural intelligence, but it will never replace the unique strengths that make us human.

Take a moment to reflect on your human needs: **What do you need to feel connected, happy, and at peace?** Is it something technology can truly offer, or is it found within you? What values do you prioritise when guiding others? And *how do your actions reflect these values?*

Leading with the Soul

When we're connected to our soul, we align with our values, and this alignment shines through in our actions. Leading from this space allows us to access our genuine selves, not a rehearsed version, but an authentic one that creates experiences with a far-reaching impact for ourselves and others.

Whether in our homes, organisations, or communities, Leading with Soul cultivates happier, more motivated individuals, stronger relationships, and more productive environments. Why? Because leading in this way builds unity, respect, and understanding. It transcends differences and promotes collective satisfaction. This way of being and model focuses on the human element in all settings, leveraging intuition and making thoughtful decisions that support well-being.

A Call for Expanded way of leading

As advanced beings, we recognise that today's world calls for an expanded, elevated version of humanity; one that integrates all parts of who we are. Leaders across all areas, whether parents, heads of corporations, or community organisers, will benefit from adopting this change.

The old days of "Do what I say, not what I do" are over. This technological world demands a higher level of consciousness from its leaders. We must replace "Because I say so" with "I will show you the way."

Nothing changes until it is perceived, making it the leader's responsibility to model the change they wish to see. By focusing on what truly matters, leaders can drive positive transformation; not just for themselves, but for everyone around them.

The Cost of Giving Up

At times, you may feel tempted to give up on your soul. Whether due to a rough patch or a persistent challenge, the struggle can feel overwhelming. When this happens, take a moment to weigh the cost of giving in.

- Remember the richness of emotional connection.
- Remember the diverse forms of intelligence you possess.
- Remember that you are capable of extraordinary things.

As scientist and educator Gregg Braden reminds us: "We are highly advanced, technologically sophisticated, soft technology." Isn't that something to be proud of?

> **We are highly advanced, technologically sophisticated, soft technology.**
> **—Gregg Braden**

Authenticity: The
Compass of Leadership

We've all heard the phrase "leading authentically," but what does it really mean?

Authenticity isn't just a trendy buzzword, it's the foundation of anything that endures. It's your home, the place where you are most coherent and natural. Everything else, the filters, the masks, the behaviors is learned. We adopt these layers to fit in, to protect ourselves, or to meet expectations that don't align with who we truly are. But being authentic means something much simpler: embracing who you are without pretending to be someone else. It's about staying true to your essence and your values, even when it's uncomfortable.

Sure, inauthenticity might bring short-term success. But ask yourself: Can it be sustained? How long can we keep the act up before cracks begin to show? Not being authentic is exhausting and unsustainable. Over time, it breeds stress, disconnection, and a sense of inner conflict. Eventually, it becomes impossible to hide the strain.

When we're not true to ourselves, it shows up in every area of our lives. Burnout, mental and physical health issues, and strained relationships—at home and at work—are all interconnected. Even when you think you're holding it all together, the loss is too great, and the pain is too real. Identify one area in your life where you are not being authentic. What's holding you back, and what's one small step you can take to change this?"

Leading from the core of who you are is about leading from within, from the inside out. It means showing up as your full self, without hiding your weaknesses or strengths. It requires transparency and genuineness. Of course, that means people will see you as you are, flaws and all. Some will like you, and some won't. But here's the thing: when you lead authentically, you earn trust. Those who follow you will do so because they believe in you, not a fake version of you. And they'll stay. They'll know you're not a fleeting act but someone with the resilience to stand the test of time.

Isn't that what we all want, to be seen as we truly are? Being our real selves is effortless. It's the natural way of being that creates results you can replicate and sustain.

What If You're Worried About Being Judged? If you're afraid of how others perceive you, take a moment to reflect: Where are you wearing masks? Are you in an environment that allows you to be yourself and are you surrounded by people who accept you for who you are?

Ask yourself this: If you can't be yourself, do you really want to be there?

When you're comfortable in your own skin, you won't need constant validation from others. True validation begins with self-acceptance, embracing both your strengths and your imperfections. This is the heart of authenticity. It's not about perfection; it's about showing up as the most coherent, truthful version of yourself. It's a way of being that transforms how you live, work, and connect.

Authenticity is your home. Come back to it.

CREATIVE ARTS: SOCIETY'S TRUTH

The following sections feature highlights from a fascinating conversation I had with Omar Meza, a producer, and CEO of DA.TE Danza, a contemporary dance company.

From the moment we met, Omar and I couldn't stop talking. Our conversation naturally flowed toward the silent language of contemporary dance. An art form that speaks volumes without a single word. We explored its transformative power, particularly in education, where it can be a vital tool to empower individuals, encouraging critical thinking and amplifying their voices in the face of adversity.

Through our discussion, we touched on the idea of using our unique gifts and emotional connections to shine a light on the often-overlooked corners of society. Omar exemplifies the essence of a Soul Leader. His mission is clear: to shed a light in society's uncomfortable truths and provoke meaningful change.

DA.TE Danza, the company Omar leads, creates, produces, and presents contemporary dance, dance theatre, and theatrical initiatives. Their work doesn't just entertain; it uses the power of art and movement as a platform for social and educational inclusion. Through creatively engaging stories, DA.TE Danza reaches audiences of all ages: babies, children, youth, and adults alike inviting reflection and conversation.

Omar's work embodies the true spirit of Leading with Soul, showing us how the arts can connect, heal, and inspire. His story serve as a powerful reminder of the impact creativity can have on society, encouraging a deeper understanding of the self and one another.

 **Talking with Omar**

Dance can't be replaced, as it is the catalyst for emotions and acts as the mirror for human beings.

AI as an Evolutionary Tool, not a Threat. It is important to identify AI as an incentive for enhancing human creativity and expression, rather than perceiving it as a replacement. While AI can certainly aid in various aspects of the scenic arts and contemporary dance, it's the intricate nuances of human emotion, interpretation, and expression that remain irreplaceable, anchoring these art forms to the essence of life itself. The collaboration between AI and artists presents exciting new possibilities and contributes to the ongoing evolution of these art forms.

Throughout history, there have been instances where the unknown (for example, the mobile phone) initially appeared as a potential threat, only to reveal itself as a source of enrichment for our expressions and the dialogues we share with the world. AI, much like the transformative shifts witnessed in the cinematic world, isn't a threat but rather a catalyst for metamorphosis. Consider the transition from silent films to the lyrical embrace of spoken words, forever altering the cinematic landscape.

Similarly, in the world of dance and theatre, the fusion of these art forms gave birth to dance/theatre, musicals, and countless interpretations that breathed new life into art. Dance, with its unique ability to capture the essence of life in the present moment, forges connections with the unseen facets of ourselves, evoking a profound sense of bliss that binds us to our humanity and emotions.

Indeed, artificial intelligence is a valuable tool, and when used ethically, there's no need to fear it. We are not solely practical beings. We are spiritual, creative, and emotional beings. In our journey through life, the touch and the presence of other humans are vital for our well-being. We thrive on connections with others, a fact of life that no machine can fully replicate. While technology may streamline tasks and even lead to changes in employment dynamics, it can never replace the unique and essential aspects of human interaction, such as empathy, understanding, and the warmth that arises from genuine connections with others.

Emotions: The Essence of Humanity

Art, particularly dance, holds a unique power to deepen the human experience, making it richer and more profoundly human.

In creative dance, the performer's movement takes precedence as the primary conveyor of the message, surpassing mere aesthetics. This physical art form connects us with touch, mobility, and emotions, grounding us in the essence of life itself. Creative dance serves as a reminder of our aliveness, evoking a range of emotions, from dreams to tears, thereby reaffirming our humanity.

The artist intention goes beyond entertainment; our aim is to unlock hearts and evoke emotions exploring deep into what makes us human. Art is a transformative experience where we see ourselves reflected in others. Just as a headmaster shapes minds and cannot be replaced, our role as Soul Leaders in the arts and the dance industry is to awaken human emotions—an essential aspect of our healthy existence.

Placement of Society's Needs at the Heart of Transformation

In contemporary dance, we aspire to activate change from a space of silence, a space where movements speak volumes and emotions reverberate.

Central to our ethos is a deep-seated respect for others and a steadfast commitment to serving our communities. When selecting themes for our social change initiatives, intuition plays a pivotal role in guiding us towards what humanity needs most at any given time. Prioritizing self-work and achieving balance in mind, body, and soul before taking the stage serves as our internal tuning fork, ensuring that our performances resonate authentically with our audience as much as society.

Our responsibility extends far beyond the boundaries of our studios or company. We hold a profound social responsibility, one that guides everything we do. Our mission transcends mere aesthetics or emotional expression; it encompasses social and educational inclusion.

A Flexible Structure

In my leadership journey, finding balance between structure and emotion wasn't a straightforward path. As a dancer, leading from emotions felt natural, but I encountered scepticism, being labelled as "too soft" and urged to adopt a more disciplined approach for business success. Initially persuaded by this advice, I shifted my focus entirely towards rigid metrics, risking my company and my connection to dance.

Fortunately, I discovered inspiration in a great and powerful artist who embodied both approaches, highlighting the crucial balance between conventional leadership and soul-led leadership. I now proudly advocate that leading with the soul is not a weakness but a strength, particularly in dance and the arts. Soul-led leadership and conventional leadership are essential, providing dancers and artists with the flexibility to be authentic while maintaining a solid foundation for focus and growth.

A flexible structure nurtures the mind, body, and soul and fosters exploration and expression in artists. A soulful leader in the arts engages in deep conversations with the audience and dancers and recognises the need for emotional freedom to produce excellence.

Simultaneously, a robust conventional structure ensures professional growth; both structures play integral roles in delivering transformative performances that impact society.

Achieving a balance is a delicate dance between structure and soul, each holding equal importance in the pursuit of artistic greatness. Embracing structure and soul in all realms of life ensures professional and personal harmony. Ongoing discipline, emotional self-management, and an understanding of our inner landscape help us navigate and make a positive impact in the world.

Nurturing Our World

In our fast-paced world, individuals and the earth need attention and care more urgently than ever. And it is for world leaders to take responsibility and transition into a new model that is sustainable with who we are.

With Soul Leaders as examples emerge new ways of thinking and new behaviours to nurture the world amidst a global mental health crisis. These leaders guide others towards introspection, sparking movement towards social change and healing. This social change promotes inclusivity and social responsibility and creates space for self-reconnection. Leaders who lead with their soul, offer new pathways to navigate today's challenges.

Consider babies whose physical needs are met but who lack affection. Without human touch, they fade away. Similarly, our world and our humanity require care and attention to thrive. Effective social strategies must address both practical and emotional needs. We must acknowledge our organic nature and the beating hearts within us. Soulful leaders can serve as remedies for collective ailments, restoring people to their essence and encouraging transformative change. This way of being cultivates a sense of connection and healing for all.

In a world intertwined with AI, the call to lead with our souls resonates as a song of love. This elevated form of human emotion guides us to become architects of our world's rejuvenation who can ensure the flourishing of individuals and the prosperity of entire communities.

Nurturing Our Souls

Whether guiding a team or navigating complex challenges, leaders must care for their well-being to effectively serve others. Soul-led leaders exemplify the resilience of the human spirit and play a pivotal role in developing community resilience.

Incorporating self-care practices into the life of a leader is essential for maintaining balance and vitality. Emotional regulation techniques such as seeking mentorship, prioritizing regular sleep, and embracing rest and rejuvenation are the foundation for well-being. Additionally, practices such as meditation, yoga, friendship, and continuous self-growth contribute to self-rejuvenation.

Creating space for creative expression and setting robust boundaries around personal time further nourish the leader's soul. These practices deepen their connection with themselves and enhance their ability to lead authentically.

Commitment to self-care cultivates resilience, and inner harmony. It equips leaders with the clarity and energy needed to positively impact their company and effectively meet the needs of those they lead.

Soul-Leading Story: The Impact of Abandoning our Soul

Years ago, I faced an unexpected challenge, a stubborn staphylococcus aureus in my ankle. This infection in the bones of the ankle joint causes pain and swelling, potentially limiting mobility. The timing of mine couldn't have been worse, as it coincided with economic and creative troubles within my dance company; we were about to release a new show. Leading under pressure in a way that did not resonate with me, I detached from my true self. I was in a dark place emotionally, and what was worse, my self-esteem was low, and I felt that I was letting everybody down. Burnout loomed on the horizon when the bacteria forced me into a hospital bed, unable to dance or walk, halting work, life, and leadership.

In that sterile environment, I found an unexpected companion. An older man abandoned by enthusiasm for life and enveloped in despair, described by his children as a bitter and unreceptive-to-talk man. I engaged with this man in conversation after a few days. As we connected as two patients needing entertainment and support, our interactions became peculiar, an intertwining of stretching exercises, shared stories, and dance moves. Through him, I saw heart poverty, sadness, scarcity in many forms, and loneliness, the abandonment of the soul. Miraculously, our connection grew stronger, and he started to change. It was then that I saw learning through him. Reconnecting with ourselves can illuminate the darkest of hearts; it transforms us.

His transformation became a mirror reflecting my own neglect and the recognition that I had abandoned my soul as well. The improvement in his emotional well-being became a light revealing the potential for change within me. It was then that I started to change the structure in my head. I worked on recognizing my inherent value as a creator, leader, and producer. In that hospital room, I resolved to reclaim myself. I envisioned a new structure for leadership, dismantling the limiting beliefs that had bound me. I embraced the conviction that my worth was more than the shadows of abandonment I had felt.

I started to exercise my leg, going up and down the hospital stairs. With every step, I noticed I was strengthening my body and spirit, simultaneously cultivating physical and emotional well-being. A wave of change surged with my newfound energy. It was then that I called my friends and surrounded myself with their warmth and support.

As things happen when we upgrade our energy, a supportive figure entered my life and helped shape the transformation at work. Together, we created a culture of seamless cohesion among purpose-driven employees, where the mission resonated with everyone. I discovered that there is no leader without a team. A leader must be well to lead, and the company's culture must be embodied by its members for resonance and harmony.

I transcended from a leader shaped by external expectations to one who led authentically. I learned that leaders hold a profound responsibility to be true to themselves and build structures that align with their essence. This shift rejuvenated me and breathed life into the company and its team. It highlighted the profound impact of leading with our souls, revealing that **true leadership, whichever form you choose, begins with being true to oneself.**

Advice for Future Leaders

Listen. Truly listen to your inner voice and the voices of those you lead. The key to unlocking what your group, your company, and the world truly need lies in actively listening to their desires and concerns.

Attain clarity about your identity and direction and acknowledge that you have come here to serve and occupy your position for a purpose which makes your value is immense. Take the time to mend what requires healing in you; then embrace it and honour it. You are the pathway that unlocks hearts, opens emotions, and brings people closer to their true selves. It's a profound responsibility that warrants acknowledgement for you stand as a catalyst for change. If you have been given the opportunity to share relevant social issues that society silences, use it as a collective voice.

Soul-Leading Thoughts

Leading with the soul isn't just important; it's a natural and nurturing approach to guiding others. In a world where mental health concerns are prevalent, soul-led leaders can reignite faith in a society that may be losing hope.

Leading with our souls isn't merely about offering structure, guidance, or understanding. Use your soul as a force for personal awakening, as it holds the extraordinary power to make a positive impact on others and heal an already vulnerable society. Leading with our souls means reconnecting with the core of our existence and our common purpose to promote justice, equality, prosperity, and well-being for all.

> **A genuine leader not only inspires but empowers others to become leaders themselves.**
> **—Omar Meza, Director, and Producer of DA.TE Danza**

A life of conscious intentions

Focusing our energy solely on one aspect of life poses the risk of upsetting our life balance and overall well-being. Caring leaders understand the importance of spreading their focus across various areas and incorporating practices that bring them joy.

We want to have rich experiences that promote both happiness and productivity. Exhausting all efforts on a singular pursuit may lead to success in that specific area, but it comes at the expense of other crucial aspects of life.

Consider the scenario of dedicating our lives solely to a particular project. When that project reaches its end, a sense of emptiness may follow. This phenomenon extends to various aspects of life. Empty nest syndrome, for instance, affects parents who have solely focused on nurturing their children. When the children eventually leave home, parents may experience sadness and a loss of purpose. Certain businesspeople who spend their entire life dedicated to their business, with no time for hobbits or friendships. When they retired many of them experience depression and emptiness.

These examples highlight the importance of intentionally creating a balanced life. One that harmonises health, work, and well-being. Life is more than a singular pursuit; it involves consciously nurturing familial, mental, emotional, and physical health, alongside moments of fun and joy. This holistic approach ensures that our leadership remains both effective and sustainable.

Guiding others can be all-consuming. Pouring our entire existence into a job may produce success, but it also carries the danger of isolating us from essential aspects of our lives. Intentionally working on life's balance is more than important, not only for the leader's sake but also for the success and happiness of those they lead.

> **The major work of the world is not done by geniuses. It is done by ordinary people, with balance in their lives, who have learned to work in an extraordinary manner.**
>
> **—Gordon B. Hinckley**

A Creative Experience: Practical Steps for Improving Life Balance

Take time to think of someone you know who lost balance in their life and where the imbalance was (for example, someone who devoted their life to looking after a parent or an ill relative).

Reflect on the consequences of putting all the eggs in one basket and what would happen if that basket were to disappear.

Take a moment to ponder this first graphic.

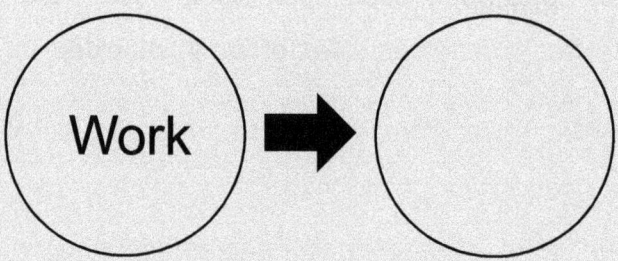

Acknowledge the potential emptiness that may arise when you invest all your attention in a single aspect of life, whether personal or professional. If you invest all your energy and attention in only one aspect (work, children), what do you have left when that fails? Think of the risks of relying solely on one thing for fulfilment.

Practise self-honesty.

Create your own graphic by honestly mapping out where your focus currently lies. Use this visual representation to identify areas where you may be overemphasizing one aspect of your life. You may use a pencil here to add the word that takes all your attention.

Explore project impact.

Reflect on the losses and challenges that may arise when a significant event or project comes to an end. Evaluate the potential impact on your life.

Embrace balanced leadership.

Refer to this third graphic as an example of a well-balanced life. Notice how productivity and fulfilment coexist. Strive for a leadership style that integrates various aspects of your life to ensure sustained success and personal satisfaction.

Family	Work	Hobbies
Exercise	Reading	Travelling
Fun	Social Life	Yoga

Create your balanced life chart.

The preceding chart might not be your thing, so using the provided blank chart, list all the crucial areas of your life that contribute to your sense of well-being, balance, fulfilment, and joy. Fill in each cell with whatever is important to you.

Apply this chart to guide your decisions and actions and thereby promote a more balanced and fulfilling life. Tend to all areas of your life, work, relationships, health, and personal growth.

The grass is greener where you water it; avoid neglecting some areas while overloading others. Take a moment today to reflect on where your attention is most needed and make the adjustments that will bring you back to equilibrium.

> **Balance is not something you find, it's something you create.**
> —Jana Kingsford, Author of Unjuggled

AI Friend or Foe

AI has quietly woven itself into the fabric of our daily lives, transforming everything from how we work to how we connect. Love it or hate it, AI is here to stay.

The friend

AI inclusion in our lives offers countless benefits, reshaping how we live, connect, and function in the modern world. From revolutionising work processes to transforming learning, travel, healthcare, and communication, AI is no longer a choice, it's a necessity. It's fascinating to watch how it evolves, changing our lives minute by minute and, let's face it, making them incredibly comfortable.

At the time of the Industrial Revolution, people viewed it as a massive threat. It brought fears of job loss and uncertainty to the surface for most. But now, think of inventions like the washing machine, dishwasher, iron, and vacuum cleaner, imagine life without them. No, thank you!

Fast-forward to today: who wouldn't love coming home to a cosy, warm house heated by an AI-powered thermostat? Or barking a quick command to Alexa, Google, or Siri and having irritating tasks taken care of effortlessly? My personal favourite is asking Alexa to set an oven timer while I write. No more burned meals while working on my book, super-efficient Alexa handles it for me. What's not to like?

Take video calls, for example. Being able to connect with my parents, siblings and their families overseas has transformed our relationships. And let's not forget the relief of no longer flipping through encyclopaedias or wrestling with foreign-language dictionaries. (Trust me, as someone who once asked for lentils in a supermarket 10 times before getting it right, I wholeheartedly embrace modern translation tools!)

Then there's the life-saving magic of tech like Apple Watches. They've become so much more than a trendy accessory. A friend of mine discovered his heart condition thanks to his watch's ECG scan. An alert prompted him to seek medical advice, ultimately saving his life. It's mind-blowing when you think about it.

And then we have ChatGPT (yes, the irony isn't lost on me). I admit, I'm a bit wary of it, but I've happily relied on it to fix my atrocious spelling, grammar, and punctuation (which, let's face it, have not improved with age). It even helped me draft the questionnaire you'll find at the end of this book. It's like a super-clever friend who shows up when you need to prepare for exams.

Let's talk about YouTube, my addiction. Whether it's learning a new recipe, fixing something around the house, watching a lecture, or indulging in guilty-pleasure cat videos, YouTube has become a go-to source of entertainment and knowledge. It's like having an endless library of tutorials and ideas at your fingertips.

And imagine what's coming next: fancy virtual reality (VR) glasses that immerse us in virtual libraries filled with millennia of wisdom. Think of the possibilities!

In the healthcare sector, AI is already a game-changer. It assists in drug discovery, optimising clinical trials, and streamlining drug manufacturing. Beyond healthcare, its influence stretches into finance, manufacturing, education, retail, agriculture, and more.

AI helps tackle complex challenges with unprecedented speed and efficiency, improving productivity and enhancing quality of life.

Will AI leave you skipping carefree through the park every afternoon? Not quite, you'll still need to work, I'm afraid. But AI can free us from mundane tasks, giving us more space to focus on creativity and innovation.

There's no doubt in my mind: AI has immense value. After all, we now live in a world where humans and technology are intertwined. Technology is neutral; it is how we utilize it that will determine what will happen to our lives. **If**—and it's a big **if**—we can regulate it ethically and maintain our boundaries, I believe we can harmonise efficiency and humanity. Yes, there will be teething problems, disruptions, and inevitable tears along the way, but I trust we'll get there.

AI can be our friend if we don't turn it into a foe. After all, it's humans who input the data and just like parents we don't let our children run the house, neither we should allow AI to run our lives.

This is the time when good parenting must take place with boundaries, integrity, and ethical codes taking precedence.

Questions to Consider: How can leaders balance the analytical capabilities of AI with human intuition?

What ethical considerations arise when integrating AI into soulful, people-centred environments?

And here's a thought to ponder:

The World Economic Forum predicts that AI could replace around 85 million jobs by 2025, but it will also create approximately 97 million new roles. This net gain underscores AI's potential to drive economic growth, diversify opportunities, and open doors to new possibilities.

The Foe

AI is, without a doubt, one of the most revolutionary developments humans have ever encountered. Its potential is staggering, and yet, we must not be blind to the challenges it brings.

The garden is not all roses, and we need to see the reality of things.

As with every great light, technology and AI cast their own shadows. Higher technology does not mean is better; is just different. If we want to shape our world and future responsibly, we must confront these shadows head-on.

History offers us lessons if we choose to learn from them. We don't want to give away our power and autonomy to the point where we become slaves.

Slaves? Yes, you read that correctly. Imagine a machine dictating your every action. That's not a sci-fi plot, it's already happening. Your smartwatch tells you to sleep two more hours, hydrate, or walk. That's all fine, right? But now imagine checking into work and being denied access because AI detects you didn't sleep enough or still have traces of Uncle Ben's birthday punch in your system. You're told you won't be paid today, nor can you return home until you've stayed to "recover" for tomorrow's optimal productivity.

Sounds ridiculous? Maybe. But it's more possible than you think. This is why boundaries are essential.

Who leads? We lead. It's up to us to stay aware, question what doesn't feel right, and maintain our freedom.

After all, AI software and robots are creations of humans. And behind those creations are people. Who are they? What are their intentions? Are these people guided by ethical principles? Are they ensuring AI serves humanity's best interests?

I choose to believe that most of these creators mean well. But even with good intentions, the implications of their innovations can spiral beyond their control. This is where ethical boundaries come in.

Unauthorized or unethical uses of AI can lead to profound consequences. From biased algorithms that perpetuate inequality in hiring or criminal justice to the creation of disturbing child-abuse content, AI misuse is a pressing concern.

Even in seemingly harmless contexts, an imbalance in human-AI collaboration can lead to heightened stress, job displacement, and a loss of human connection. If we're not careful, we risk detaching from our messy, wonderful emotions; the very thing that makes us human.

Mo Gawdat, former chief business officer of Google X, predicted that AI would double human capabilities by 2029 and now says it will happen much sooner. This acceleration demands answers to these questions:

Can we regulate something that's potentially smarter than us? How much AI do we want in our lives? How much of our freedom are we willing to give away? These are not just philosophical musings. They are the questions we must answer now, while we still hold the reins.

A Social Experiment Worth Trying

When I shared these insights with my friend Hannah, a leadership coach, she told me about an eye-opening experiment she ran with her students to explore their relationship with technology, specifically, their phones.

Hannah noticed her students were glued to their devices in class. The moment they sat down, out came the phones, placed on desks like lifelines. Many couldn't function without them, and she suspected this constant attachment was contributing to heightened anxiety and mental health issues.

For her stress workshop, Hannah conducted a simple social experiment. She first asked students to rate their stress levels, which were relatively low. Then, she asked them to place their phones on their desks, collected them in a box, and informed them they wouldn't get them back until the end of the three-hour session.

Some students were fine with it. Others protested loudly, despite having consented beforehand. Some panicked when they realised, they couldn't access their phones during the session. After this, Hannah asked them to rate their anxiety and stress levels again, almost all of them reported higher scores.

She decided to make the break longer, 30 minutes instead of the usual 15 and encouraged the students to talk to each other. Despite initial resistance and excuses to retrieve their phones, most students eventually settled into conversations.

By the end of the workshop, stress levels had dropped significantly. Students admitted they felt more sociable and less anxious without their phones. Many noted they had started using their phones less frequently after the experiment, choosing to be more present in certain situations.

Hannah's experiment highlighted a profound truth: while phones and technology give us the illusion of connection, they can also increase anxiety and rob us of the joy of the present moment.

It's a powerful reminder to be mindful of how technology affects our well-being and to make intentional choices that enrich our lives.

Symptoms of a larger issue

We all know by now how phones disrupt social interactions. I can't help but notice shop assistants sitting in the back, scrolling through their phones, not even greeting customers. It breaks my heart and my patience.

This is why I refuse to stay in businesses where staff choose screens over service. This isn't just about one bad habit: it's a symptom of a larger issue. Technology has the power to make life easier, but it also risks making it poorer in terms of genuine enjoyment and connection.

We must ask ourselves: What do we want from our lives and businesses? How much technology do we need, and where do we draw the line?

The path forward

AI offers intelligence beyond our wildest imagination, but it lacks the depth of human experience and emotion. It's up to us to ensure that technological advancements serve humanity, rather than overshadow it.

Let's embrace AI as a tool, not a master. By staying united, ethical, and intentional, we can ensure a future where technology supports us without eroding the qualities that make us truly human.

> **It is the responsibility of leadership to work intelligently with what is given, and not waste time fantasizing about a world of flawless people and perfect choices.**
>
> **—Marcus Aurelius**

INSIGHTS FROM SUCCESSFUL LEADERS

Have you ever wondered what it takes to be a successful leader? Through conversations with leaders who have navigated various organisational backgrounds, I've gained insights that can apply to every aspect of life. These insights extend far beyond the confines of corporate boardrooms, offering timeless wisdom that we can all benefit from in any area.

People at the centre

A leader must prioritise the well-being and development of team members. When individuals feel valued, they're more likely to be motivated and committed to achieving shared goals. Taking the time to listen to their concerns, recognise their contributions, and provide support when needed can go a long way in cultivating a positive and productive environment.

Know Alignment Is Key

In any collaborative effort, regardless of the task at hand, alignment among team members is essential for success. When everyone is working towards the same dreams and objectives, there is a sense of unity and cohesion. Ensuring that everyone understands their role and how it contributes to the overall mission helps avoid many misunderstandings and pitfalls.

Reject Individualism

In any team setting, whether at home or at work, individualism can be damaging to overall functioning and morale. When team members are self- absorbed in their self-interests over collective goals, resentment, conflict, and a lack of trust can arise. A mindset of curiosity, collaboration, and cooperation, where everyone works together towards a common purpose, is essential for building a cohesive and effective team.

Cultivate Collaboration

Look for signs of collaboration, openness, and inclusivity. Before committing to joining a team, club, or community, take time to assess its culture and values to see if they align with yours. Don't be too eager to mould yourself; consider whether you are in the right place with the right people.

A culture that values teamwork and mutual support is more likely to encourage creativity, innovation, and success. When we align ourselves with like-minded individuals, we create positive and enriching spaces for growth and development.

Spot Potential Soul Leaders

Keep an eye out for individuals who demonstrate qualities of soulful leadership. These may include initiative other's awareness, resilience, and a commitment to serving others.

When you encounter a potential Soul Leader, celebrate their achievements, provide mentorship, and empower them to make a positive difference in their world. They need you as much as you need them!

Happiness Drives Well-Being and Productivity

Happiness isn't just a fleeting emotion, it's a powerful force influencing every aspect of life. Whether we're a leader or part of a team, at home or in the workplace, our level of happiness and the quality of our interactions with others play significant roles in shaping our experiences.

Imagine a team where every member feels valued, supported, and appreciated. Team members enjoy positive relationships with their colleagues and share a sense of camaraderie and purpose. In this environment, happiness overflows, leading to improved confidence, lower stress levels, and greater overall well-being.

Now, let's look at the impact on productivity. When team members are happy and fulfilled, they're more likely to be motivated, creative, and focused on achieving their goals.

They collaborate more effectively, communicate openly, and contribute their best ideas and efforts to the team. As a result, productivity soars, and the quality of work produced is consistently high.

When we intentionally place humans at the centre of our focus, the well-being of every individual is a top priority. Leaders who place their team members' happiness and fulfilment at the centre create a ripple effect of positivity that benefits everyone involved.

From improved social interactions to enhanced well-being and higher-quality output, the benefits of happiness in soul-led environments are undeniable. This applies to the home environment too.

Corporations: Blending Heart and Strategy

Francesca Hamptons, Group CFO at Raymond James Wealth and Management, is someone I could speak about endlessly. She's a natural-born leader who seamlessly combines sharp business skills with genuine humanity, a rare blend that sets her apart and emphasises her success. Francesca's ability to bridge emotions and intelligence with effortless grace is nothing short of remarkable.

During her interview for this book, Francesca shared these profound words: "Leading is a dual-edged sword; it's a privilege, yet it carries a weighty burden."

In that moment, it became clear that for Francesca, leading with the soul isn't just a professional role; it's something she fully embraces and embodies.

Her leadership exemplifies the essence of soul-led leadership. She understands that true leadership is not defined by position or hierarchy. Instead, as Francesca demonstrates, it is a state of being one that invites connection, purpose, and alignment with values.

Talking with Francesca

A leader can learn a variety of leadership skills from scratch and deliver good results by studying the art of delegation, stakeholder management, and process delivery, to name but a few.

True leadership, however, is more than just carrying out tasks and processes; it is inspiring a group of individuals and understanding the team's needs and the unique reasons each individual is there. This understanding helps you connect with them on a personal level. As important as this is, showing the team who you are is equally important so they can feel at ease in communicating with you authentically; creating a trusting environment is crucial to leading well.

When you are leading with your soul, you're not just focused on getting the job done; you're committed to bringing out the best in each person, both professionally and personally. The results speak for themselves: happy, fulfilled individuals who are naturally more productive and resilient in the face of challenges. It creates a team dynamic filled with energy and support for one another.

This model requires time, emotional energy, and investment, the outcomes are rewarding and can achieve better performance alongside increased productivity, well-being, and contentment. People feel understood, valued, and supported, producing results that don't just meet expectations but exceed them, and the individual, the team, and the company flourish.

Leading from a place of alignment and congruence requires a deep understanding of each individual, their vulnerabilities, weaknesses, and strengths. It is our job to adapt our responsiveness to their needs. In return, people follow and respect you as a leader and eagerly embark on the next journey, the next project, together. This level of commitment and engagement is much harder to achieve through transactional leadership alone.

Benefits of Having More Leaders who Lead with their Souls within Corporations

Engagement Generates Higher Returns

When you have a compassionate leader at the helm, something powerful happens. People feel more than just motivated, they feel truly engaged and responsive. It isn't a culture where everyone's just going through the motions to check boxes on a survey, worried about the implications. No, this is a culture built on authenticity, where people genuinely care about each other, and care about the work they're doing.

This level of engagement leads to higher returns, not just in productivity and profitability but also in overall satisfaction and fulfilment. These are some of the benefits of having Soul Leaders in charge.

Success in this position isn't just about holding a title, it's about embodying a genuine passion for the work you do. Leaders who align with the organisation's purpose, and who approach their responsibilities with personal energy, create a culture of engagement and increased potential for growth.

And here's the thing: leadership isn't always smooth sailing. It involves making tough decisions, like acquiring or letting go of companies or parting ways with team members. Amidst these challenges, what truly determines success is your unwavering passion for the job.

Whether you're a natural risk-taker or you have learned to embrace uncertainty through experiences and conditioning, your genuine love for what you do is what ultimately shines through in your leadership. When you're not genuinely loving what you're doing and you're not finding purpose in it, it reflects in your work and how you lead others. Without that passion, connections with your team won't be genuine, and their ability to succeed will suffer.

The beauty of leadership lies in witnessing the growth and success of those you lead. To facilitate that growth, you must genuinely care about your team and your work. And it is for you to find a way to let them know you have their backs and are there to support them, even in the face of risk and uncertainty.

Shawn Anchor, best-selling author of The Happiness Advantage and chief experience officer for Better Up, writes the following in an article published in the Harvard Business Review: *Job satisfaction is not only the key predictor of turnover rates. In The Happiness Advantage, I make the research case for the fact that the single greatest advantage in the modern economy is a happy and engaged workforce. A decade of research proves that happiness raises nearly every business and educational outcome: raising sales by 37%, productivity by 31%, and accuracy on tasks by 19%, as well as a myriad of health and quality of life improvements.*

In other words, investing in happiness pays great dividends. For the full article and report, consult this book's list of references.

The role of those in leadership and what truly entails success in this role hinges on your genuine passion for the job.

> **Leadership It's about communication between people …the rest is technology.**
> **—Hans Vestberg, Former CEO of Ericsson**

Leadership Isn't One-Size-Fits-All
(A Role Beyond Description)

Leadership isn't one-size-fits-all, nor is it about possessing specific skills. It's about having a true desire to lead. And if that desire isn't there, that's perfectly okay. Not everyone is born to be a leader, and it's something to embrace rather than resist.

If you choose to step into a leadership role, you have to be prepared for the large dose of responsibility and accountability it carries. This role entails a lot more than just delivering against a job description. You will have to make tough decisions, put in extra hours, and ultimately prioritise the well-being of the people you lead.

In essence, this role will put a weighty responsibility on your shoulders that goes beyond the job description or role title. It is your job to shoulder that responsibility with compassion and integrity, knowing that your actions will impact the lives of those you lead.

You've got to be ready to do extraordinary things, not just for the company's benefit but for the people you're leading. Leadership, and leading with a soul, is a journey filled with many challenges, but also incredibly rewarding when approached with authenticity and care.

Embrace your potential, even when it comes from unexpected sources

Are leaders born with this ability or made? Who sees the ability to lead first, the person or those observing the person?

Growing up I never saw myself as a natural leader. I realised later in life that I had possessed some natural leadership skills as a child.

I stumbled upon clues in my old school reports after my mother passed away. It was then that I saw how being a leader had been a part of my makeup all along. At that young age, leadership had a different meaning for me.

I loved organizing others, from orchestrating charity efforts to rallying classmates for common reasons. I loved getting people together for a good cause. The signs were there; I just hadn't noticed them.

In school sports, where I found myself in a defensive position rather than in the spotlight, I never had the glory of shooting goals, but I did tend to encourage the team from the back. The teachers observing me somehow saw leadership potential and appointed me as captain. I initially wasn't thrilled, but looking back, it makes sense; if I could lead the team from the back then, I must have had some inspiring skills.

After school, my leadership journey continued into my accounting career. Even though I wasn't actively seeking leadership roles, life had other plans for me.

In my mid-twenties, I unexpectedly stepped into a managerial role in banking after just four weeks of being there, following the unexpected departure of my boss. I was anxious but I took the opportunity. That job was followed by a two-year stint in a consultancy team. It was in this job that I gained invaluable skills in company restructuring.

It was during my stint with the consultancy team, other people began to recognise qualities in me that I hadn't fully acknowledged. As we were reshaping the company, the opportunity arose to apply for a finance director role. A consultant asked me if I was going to apply for it. I was taken aback; I hadn't considered it. I was still young, and my intention was to leave and become a consultant, a role I was enjoying. Yet, their encouragement and belief in my abilities prompted me to reconsider.

Over the years, I have worked intensively to hone the skills and resilience necessary to be a good leader, so answering the question of whether leaders are born or made, it all depends. In some cases, nature and nurture apply, like in my case; in others, it is the result of working hard, learning, and taking on the environment.

What I've come to know is that leadership isn't always something you see in yourself. Sometimes, it takes the keen eyes of those around you to spot the qualities that make you a leader. Beyond mere skills, true leadership encompasses qualities like listening, risk management, a thirst for continuous learning, and a willingness to embrace unexpected opportunities.

So, whether you believe leaders are born or made, one thing is clear: the leadership journey is often filled with surprises, challenges, and moments of self-discovery. It's about recognizing and embracing your potential, even when it comes from unexpected sources.

 **Soul-Leading Story: True Leadership demands Empathy and Connection**

Early on in my career, I had an eye-opening moment of leadership. It wasn't just about delivering performance and navigating corporate labyrinths; it was about people, their emotions, their livelihoods. It was a revelation which occurred during a tough restructuring I was leading. I had to make decisions that would impact the lives of a team, and although this is always difficult, this team that had been together for years.

I thought I had everything planned out perfectly, following every HR protocol to support the impact this

Leading with Soul

restructuring was going to have on their work. But in the heat of the moment, I realised it was more than just ticking boxes. People's lives were at stake. Some were facing uncertainty, while others saw new opportunities.

As I gathered my thoughts, it became clear to me that what they needed wasn't a rehearsed corporate speech; they needed genuine empathy, a human touch, to know that they weren't just expendable assets so they could leave the organisation with a positive feeling.

So, I took a step back and put myself in their shoes. I listened, absorbed, and tried to respond to their needs. It was scary, yes, but I knew I had to stay calm and positive for them. Through it all, I learned that true leadership demands empathy and connection.

Fast-forward ten years, and I faced another large restructuring. I approached it with the same ethos. Every individual mattered, and this time, with some learnings in me, it wasn't just about minimizing impacts; it was about empowering them for what lay ahead. I made sure each person had support, coaching, and a soft landing into their new future.

Seeing the gratitude from those who felt genuinely cared for during such a tough time was humbling, which was ironic, as we are supposed to look after them all the time. It reminded me that leading people isn't about ego; it's about serving others, nurturing relationships, and inspiring trust.

Leadership can be daunting, especially in tough times, but it's a privilege. It's about embracing vulnerability, compassion, and a commitment to serve others and their well-being so we can be the kind of leaders' people choose to follow not because of authority, but because of inspiration.

Unfortunately, too many potentially good leaders let their egos overshadow their ability to connect with and support their team. It's those who truly embody soulful leadership and make a difference that is felt.

Advice for Future Leaders: Reflect on whether leading others brings you genuine happiness and fulfilment.

Leading is a dual-edged sword; t's a privilege, yet it carries a weighty burden.

Before stepping into the role, take the time to deeply understand what it entails, as it significantly impacts your own life and the lives of those you lead. Leadership extends far beyond the confines of the organisation.

Reflect on whether leading others brings you genuine happiness and fulfilment. Are you in the right place, aligned with the place goals and values?

Authenticity is key; when leaders prioritise their agendas over the collective good, it doesn't go unnoticed. Despite attempts to conceal true intentions, they often become blatantly obvious, sparking conversation and speculation within the organisation.

Soul-Leading Thoughts

The reasons behind assuming leadership profoundly impact both tangible and intangible returns. Ask yourself: are you stepping into this role for the right reasons? Are you truly passionate about leading and committed to improving the company and its people?

Your answers will shape outcomes not only for yourself but also for the organisation and those within it. Leadership is about creating a positive ripple effect that benefits both the organisation and its people. Take a moment to reflect and ensure your intentions align with the greater good.

> **Raise your message, not your voice.**
> **—Danelle Delgado, CEO**
> **of Life Intended**

A Creative Experience for Defining What Matters Most

This exercise helps you clarify your priorities, reduce stress, and align your leadership journey with your core values.

Steps:

Prepare Yourself:

Find a quiet, comfortable space where you can focus without interruptions. Have a journal or notepad ready to write down your thoughts.

Reflect on Your Priorities:

- What is most important to you right now?
- Which aspects of your life bring you the greatest sense of purpose, joy, or fulfilment?
  Write down your answers without overthinking.

Identify Non-Negotiables:

- What are the boundaries or commitments you refuse to compromise?

- These might include personal time, family commitments, self-care, or workplace values. Be specific. For example, "Prioritizing 30 minutes of reflection daily" or "Ensuring weekends are dedicated to family."

Set Boundaries with Clarity:

- Think about areas in your life where you need to say no to protect your priorities.
- Write down one or two ways you can communicate these boundaries clearly and respectfully, using "I" statements.

Visualize the Results:

- Close your eyes and imagine your life with these boundaries in place.
- How does it feel? What changes do you notice in your stress levels, relationships, or leadership style?

Take Small, Focused Actions:

- Commit to one small adjustment this week that supports your priorities.
- For example, "I will block time on my calendar for reflection" or "I will delegate one work task that doesn't align with my values."

After completing this exercise, revisit your notes in a few days or weeks. Ask yourself:

- Are these boundaries helping me stay aligned with what matters most?
- What adjustments can I make to ensure I'm honouring my priorities consistently?

This practice is not just about saying no; it's about creating the space to say yes to what truly matters.

> **Good boundaries, both those that help us manage ourselves and lead others, always produce freedom, not control.**
> **—Henry Cloud**

COHERENT JOURNEY

Why Is Using Your Natural Abilities Key for a Coherent Leadership Journey. Ever find yourself trying to lead like someone else, only to end up exhausted and doubting every decision? The path of leading others can feel like a maze of challenges, filled with trials, errors, and constant self-corrections.

Most of us have stopped to watch a video, conference, or think of a parent that demonstrate what we think is the successful version of ourselves. It's tempting to look to others for guidance, to follow their paths in the hope they'll lead us to success. But here's the thing: leadership isn't one-size-fits-all and pretending it is, can drain us.

The Trap of Copying Others

When we try to adopt someone else's methods, we overlook a crucial fact: we're not them. We don't share the same DNA, resilience, or way of processing the world. Yet we eagerly listen to advice on how to lead, sidelining our own instincts, our own inner essence; the voice that truly knows what resonates with who we are.

Ignoring that voice can lead us to use scripts and behaviors that don't fit. Eventually, impostor syndrome sneaks in, casting doubt on every decision we make. Thanks, impostor syndrome, you're about as welcome as a rainy day at a picnic. This self-doubt builds stress, exhaustion, and disconnects us from our natural strengths. Suddenly, we're not just off track; we're on a fast path to burnout.

The Cost of Ignoring Your Inner Voice

Burnout isn't just an emotional toll. When we lose touch with ourselves, the costs pile up, like a game of Jenga on the verge of collapse. Teams or household members become disengaged, relationships suffer, and the coherence in our work dissolves. It can feel like we're trapped in a comedy of errors, except the punchline is lost.

If we're fortunate, someone might nudge us back toward our own strengths with a gentle reminder to "be yourself." If we're listening, this advice can be the turning point, sadly most of the time we don't listen. When we do, we embrace our natural abilities becoming more than just leaders, we become authentic people with the power to connect and inspire from a place of truth.

The Rise of the Natural Leader

Leading in a way that feels coherent begins with communicating simply, clearly, and in a way that aligns with your true self. Instead of wasting years copying others or rehearsing lines in the mirror, tap into your unique strengths. Practice agile, honest communication that comes from the heart. Seek out a mentor or coach who can help you uncover your hidden talents and turn them into assets and most important, take feedback.

When you bring your heart and soul into your daily activities, you celebrate what comes naturally to you and that's where leading from an authentic place begins. You tap into your abilities, and the natural leader within you shines. You're no longer an impostor or an imitation; you're a true leader, grounded in who you are.

Trusting your natural abilities might seem risky at first. But the rewards, both for you and for those you lead, are worth it. When you lead from a place of coherence and congruency, your best self emerges effortlessly. You create a path that others want to follow, not because of where it leads, but because of how genuine and inspiring the journey feels.

Is the Definition of Success Shifting?

For years, success has often been defined by financial wealth, professional achievements, or the sheer number of projects completed. But as the world changes, so does our understanding of what it means to lead a fulfilling life. Today, success feels less like a fixed destination and more like a fluid concept, one that can shift to reflect our evolving values and priorities.

To discover what success means to you right now, begin by asking yourself, "What does success mean to me?" It's a big question, I know, and it may lead to even more questions. But it is through exploring these possibilities and bringing them to our consciousness that we unlock the potential for richer, more meaningful lives. Whether it's gaining recognition, achieving financial stability, finding joy, or hitting specific milestones, take a close look at why these things matter to you.

Consider what it will take to reach your goals and, perhaps more importantly, what it will take to sustain them. Are your heart and soul truly satisfied with the sacrifices involved?

Take a minute to think what effect your success will have on you and others and what the potential loses could be. Does this vision improve your life and the lives of others? If not, it may be worth reconsidering what impact it might have on you and them. Difficult decisions I know, but better to make them before they become regrets.

Choose your difficult and once you have chosen, don't look back.

A friend of mine has a poster in his house that reads: 'On the way to a dream, I found a better one.' For years, I pondered its meaning without fully understanding it. Then one day, it became clear: as we journey through life, our priorities naturally evolve, leading us to unexpected and perhaps more meaningful destinations.

While financial stability remains important, our concept of achievement often grows to encompass more meaningful pursuits. Many of us have heard stories of people who reached the pinnacle of their careers or accumulated wealth, only to feel unfulfilled. In their climb to the top, they sometimes lost sight of what truly mattered, becoming disconnected from themselves and those around them. These stories are powerful reminders that success isn't just about reaching a goal; it's about finding purpose and alignment along the way.

Increasingly, success is being redefined to include values beyond financial security. It's about building positive relationships, contributing to communities, nurturing loved ones, and caring for the environment.

Whatever your own version of success looks like, make sure it resonates with your core self. Let it be your choice, not the expectations of parents, neighbours, or friends.

Ultimately, success should be a source of fulfilment, not a checklist imposed by others. Take the time needed to define what success truly means to you, and make sure it's a definition that honours your values, your relationships, and your well-being. That way, you can move forward with confidence, knowing that your achievements reflect the person you genuinely are and want to be.

Entrepreneurship: Juggling
Different Huts

I first met Sam Thomas, the co-founder of County Business Clubs, host of the Different Hats podcast, managing director of SBT, and owner of Firm Balls, at a charity dinner through a mutual friend. From the outset, his remarkable ability to foster genuine connections stood out. Whether at events, in his podcast, or in business settings, Sam has a natural gift for making people feel valued and included.

Sam is the type of leader who doesn't just talk, he takes action for others. Listening to his podcast, I was struck by how his questions weren't just polished or rehearsed; they were authentic, heartfelt, and genuinely curious.

As someone whose actions align so closely with his words, Sam is a soulful leader who walks his talk. Naturally, I wanted to interview him for this book. There was no formal setup, just a casual coffee chat in my kitchen, free of scripts or filters.

"What makes your conversations with people so successful?" I asked him.

His response was immediate and profound: "I bring my soul into the conversations we have."

Wow! I thought.

What followed was an open, flowing discussion that felt timeless. Hours had slipped by unnoticed. Sam's insights, shaped by his roles as a digital creator, podcaster, entrepreneur, and businessman, are included in the following sections. His thoughtful approach serves as a powerful example of how leading with the soul can transcend industries and create profound, lasting impact.

Talking with Sam

From an early age, my fascination with people and profound connections seamlessly intertwined with my passion for business.

My love for people led me to the vibrant world of the hair industry, managing salons for TONI&GUY. Surrounded by incredible individuals, I absorbed invaluable lessons. However, my trajectory shifted when influenced by external pressures, I began prioritizing money over authentic connections. Inadvertently, I adopted a boss mentality, neglecting the essence of true leadership.

The repercussions were swift. I lost touch with my audience, and the disconnect permeated my work. Struggling with this new mindset, I faced losses, including financial setbacks.

That pivotal moment prompted a promise to myself: my next venture would harness my innate ability to connect authentically. I vowed to cultivate an environment where people felt comfortable being vulnerable, where I would actively participate in the culture, and where I would explore my innate abilities to connect others and make business.

Subsequent businesses, still thriving, reflected this commitment. Among them, podcasting emerged as a personal favourite.

Embrace Vulnerability as a Strength to Transform Conversations, and Cultivate Openness in Others

My insatiable curiosity and love for learning found a home in podcast conversations. While delving into others' stories and journeys, my genuine interest encouraged openness. This mutual exchange became a cathartic experience, offering an education unlike any other.

In these conversations, I confront topics I, at times, find challenging. This dynamic process allows me to learn while indulging in my passion, connecting with people, and infusing authenticity into our discussions. The result is genuine, open, and vulnerable exchanges, creating an impact that goes beyond words. A transformational experience for all involved.

What came as a common thread in most of the episodes I have recorded, is that we are here to love and be loved.

Bringing my soul into conversations helps others to open and be vulnerable. And this vulnerability is a strength that has the power to transform what we can achieve and do for ourselves and others.

These days, I remember to keep authentic using my natural abilities, connecting with the human in me who sees and honours the human in the other person.

Are we still stuck in outdated leadership models, or are we witnessing an evolution towards soulful leadership?

In these pivotal years since the pandemic, a noticeable surge towards soulful leadership has caught my attention. When the pandemic happened, we all understood very quickly what was working and what wasn't in our lives. Who was in our journey to stay and who wasn't. We also saw a vast number of leaders working relentlessly with their hearts and souls for others even though their own well-being was at risk.

We rediscovered then what truly brings us happiness; the lack of freedom and countless challenges we faced changed our perspective on what truly mattered. The seismic shifts of COVID-19 crystallized the imperative need to be true to ourselves, an understanding best achieved through vulnerable conversations.

We were called for change at all levels, emphasizing the urgency of transitioning from traditional leadership models to a more soulful, authentic approach. As a result of all of this, there is now a collective yearning for more meaningful conversations.

I firmly believe that this seismic event helped with the rise of people who now choose to lead with the soul and not just the intellect.

Soulful leaders exist in greater numbers than we might acknowledge, and the pandemic has acted as a catalyst for this change, prompting introspection and a profound revaluation of priorities. While we may not have fully embraced this transformation, the momentum is unmistakable.

There Are No Euphoric Moments, Just an Ongoing Journey of Fulfilment

Fulfilment isn't about a single euphoric moment; it's an ongoing journey. In my conversations with diverse leaders, ranging from Olympians to seasoned entrepreneurs, a common revelation emerged, the absence of a gold moment.

Many recognised that reaching their goals didn't usher in a magical experience. Some had to move the goalpost or shift their goals, while others sought something deeper fulfilment. And that fulfilment, they discovered, was found not in the achievements, but in the shared experiences and genuine happiness of their teams and families.

COVID acted as a catalyst for this realisation, particularly for businesspeople accustomed to the daily hustle outside. Deprived of constant human connection during the pandemic, they unearthed a profound truth: it wasn't just about money; it was about human connection and meaningful interactions.

In an unexpected way, the pandemic became a powerful force that brought us back home to what truly matters. It serves as a reminder that amidst life's pursuits, the essence of happiness lies in the simplicity of shared moments.

This pivotal shift in perspective marks the commencement of a journey back to ourselves. The stories shared by these leaders I met, resonate with a universal truth, happiness lies in the small, everyday interactions and shared joys with those that matter.

Self-Care Isn't a Luxury; It's a Lifeline

Risking who you truly are means not accomplishing what your heart desires. If we don't stop and look after ourselves, we are never going to be the best version of ourselves so the world won't enjoy all we can give.

As an entrepreneur, you feel that you always must be productive, that you have to be so many things to so many people, bearing the weight of countless roles with commitments piling on.

We often put ourselves last, believing our commitments come first, until one day, reality hits: without us, everything halts. We wear so many different hats that if we don't take time for self-care, we run the risk of developing multiple personality disorder. It hit me; neglecting this crucial time for myself risked losing who I truly am and not fulfilling my desires. I now know, that Ignoring self-care can lead to losing touch with our purpose.

Recently, I found solace in self-care and meditation.

In the chaos, remember self-care isn't a luxury; it's a lifeline. It's about more than being a better leader; it's about being the best version of yourself. Without this pause, the world misses out on the real you.

Take time to self-care, not just for you, but for the profound impact it has on those you lead and the world that deserves the best version of you.

Connection is why we are here; it is what gives us purpose and meaning to our lives.

—Brené Brown

 **Soul-Leading Story: Measure Success Differently**

I remember the biggest turning point for me so far was turning forty. I hit the realisation that for a long time, I had been driven by money, and despite that, I was far from the millionaire I wanted to become. I could not give my children the life I imagined for them, and I felt like a failure.

From that moment, I went from being a very positive person most of the time to being in the dark. I was questioning a lot about what I was doing, and my mental health started suffering; searching inside myself for my soul, I questioned everything.

In that soul search, I noticed that most of my beliefs were tied to money and not to living an authentic life. And the life I wanted to give to my children was all tied to beliefs around money, when all my children wanted was connection and love. That is why we are here, to love and to be loved.

What got me through this darkness was the thought that if I were to die tomorrow, I would be surrounded by people who loved me. Wow! I thought.

The relationships I have with my parents, siblings, and friends are very positive, and that is success in its own right. I know they are there for me and I am there for them, I concluded realising that I was surrounded by love. And so, I began to use this metric as a measure of success.

The metric by which I measure my success today is based on the relationships I have built and the connections I have. This way of measuring success supported me to come out of the dark space, restore the connection with my soul, and change the narrative in my head of how to measure success. Hence the podcast is tied to seeing success differently.

We are still in a society that measures success based on financial status and external validation. It was my driver, and goal too, for far too long, and is something I'd like to change. When you take a step back, you realise that money is not a healthy driver for everyone. And so, in my podcast, I am changing that narrative.

Since then, it has been my mission to change the way we lead, connect, and make money.

Of course, money is very important to survive, and money is good, but the way we lead must come from a deeper place.

When you are struggling financially, it is difficult to see the benefits of another way to lead; there is a balance to be had. But I do believe that if you believe in yourself and are aligned with your purpose, values, and mission as well as surrounding yourself with the right people, you will get through.

The belief in what I am doing, and the place where this purpose comes from, will bring the money as a by-product of what I am doing, but it won't be the goal. It is not about the money anymore.

In the podcast, I have these incredible conversations where I engage with people on entirely new levels I've never experience before. The stories of my podcast guests, their journeys, and reflections on how they now see success, are confirming that happiness in who we are and what we do is the key to success.

> **Success is not the key to happiness. Happiness is the key to success. If you love what you are doing, you will be successful.**
> **—Albert Schweitzer**

Advice for Future Entrepreneurs: Connect with Your Natural Abilities

If you're venturing into the entrepreneurial field, first and foremost, connect with your natural abilities.

Your unique skills and talents are your greatest assets. By tapping into them, you can unlock a deeper level of happiness and fulfilment in your work.

Trust in your abilities and allow them to guide you as you navigate the challenges and opportunities of entrepreneurship.

Next, take the time to connect with the compelling reasons behind your journey. What impact do you want to make? What change do you hope to see in the world? Understanding your why (purpose and motivation) will fuel your drive and determination as you strive to achieve what you want.

Reflect on why you are the right person for the job, and then believe in yourself and in your ability to make a difference.

Ultimately, remember that it is not just about achieving success; it's about making a meaningful impact. Stay true to yourself, stay connected to your purpose, and let your natural abilities guide you towards success and fulfilment in the entrepreneurial field.

Soul-Leading Thoughts

It's time for a shift, a journey back to our authentic selves, where genuine connection thrives.

In today's fast-paced world, it's easy to get caught up in the hustle and bustle, losing sight of what truly matters. But deep within us, there's a yearning for something more meaningful, something real.

Leading with Soul invites us to rediscover our true essence and lead with sincerity and vulnerability. It's about embracing our humanity, with all its imperfections, and letting that sincerity shape our interactions and relationships.

So, let's make the shift, showing up as our true selves, and in doing so, we invite others to do the same. It's in these moments of vulnerability and authenticity that true connection is born.

> **Clarity leads to attention and attention leads to results.**
> **—Henry Cloud**

A Creative Experience: Stay True to Your Initial Intentions

Do you remember where you're headed and why? This experience is designed to help you regularly reassess and reaffirm your purpose, ensuring you stay true to your original intentions. As a leader, navigating the challenges of leadership becomes far easier when you have clarity about your goals and values. People who reflect consistently on their journeys are better equipped to adapt, overcome challenges, and create meaningful impact.

When we first take on the responsibility of guiding others, we often do so with compelling reasons that light the way. But then life happens. Things get busy, chaotic even. It's easy to get sidetracked, to lose sight of the destination we were sailing towards or worse, to feel like we're adrift without a compass.

Yet, clarity can anchor us. When we know what we're doing, the impact we desire to have, the changes we aim to create, and most importantly, why we're doing it, staying focused becomes much easier. This exercise invites you to reflect on your journey as a leader and ensure you're aligned with your deepest intentions. It's not just about navigating through challenges; it's about steering your ship toward a destination that truly matters.

Below, you'll find a reflective tool we'll call the "Logical Levels of Excellence." This simple but powerful framework helps you chart your course, keeping your leadership grounded in clarity and in the right direction.

Take a few moments to answer the questions associated with each level of the pyramid. Write them down here, or if you prefer, replicate the chart, and place it somewhere visible: in your office, home, or workplace. By making these intentions tangible and present, you'll have a constant reminder of your direction and progress.

Mission and Vision:

What greater purpose drives me as a leader? What impact do I want to create in my community, place of work, or family?

Values:

What are the core values I stand by, even when the waters get rough? How do these values show up in my decisions and actions?

Goals:

What are my tangible goals as a leader? What does success look like, both for me and those I guide?

Behaviours and Actions:

What daily actions do I take to reflect my values and move closer to my goals? Am I leading by example in a way that inspires trust and collaboration?

Environment and Culture:

What kind of environment am I creating for those I lead? Does it foster growth, trust, and alignment with our shared mission? I suggest you ask your questions from the bottom up.

After completing the pyramid, step back and observe your answers. Do you feel aligned with your soul's essence as a leader? Are there adjustments you'd like to make?

Use this exercise as a regular check-in and remember that leadership is a journey, not a destination.

When your actions stem from a deeper alignment with your purpose, you'll not only navigate challenges with clarity but also inspire others to join you on a path that resonates with their own values.

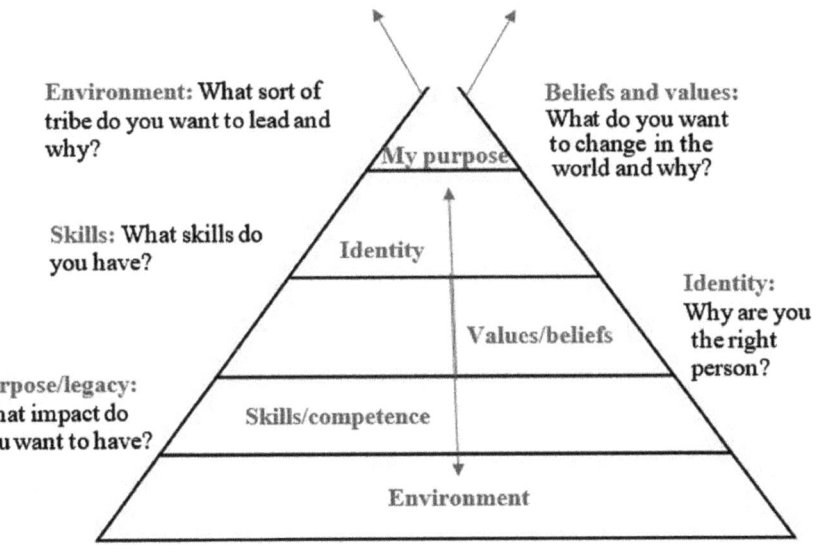

Leaders Connected to a Higher Purpose

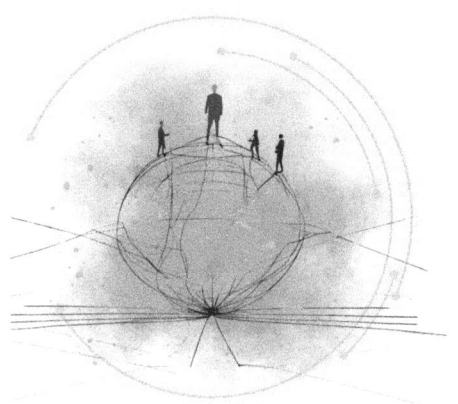

Leaders connected to a higher purpose radiate distinctive qualities. Beyond the natural traits of someone who leads with soul, these individuals embody virtues like humility, gratitude, and a deep commitment to noble intentions.

Their goal isn't simply to guide people from point A to point B; instead, they embark on a journey fuelled by a deeper calling. Even when the road ahead is unclear, they remain steadfast, anchored by their mission, values, and unwavering sense of purpose. This grounding naturally draws others to them, inspired not only by the leader but by the shared vision they represent.

These leaders focus not just on the destination but on the journey itself.

They embrace the process because they believe in the goodness of what they are working to achieve not just for themselves, but for others, and sometimes for the whole of humanity.

Their leadership is an invitation to join them, not for the destination alone, but for the shared purpose that resonates deeply in the hearts of those who follow.

Witnessing this kind of leadership is a powerful reminder: when we align ourselves with a mission greater than our own, we create a path that uplifts everyone it touches. That thought truly makes my heart sing.

Charity: Turning pain into purpose

The following text comes from a conversation I had with Dr. Zareen Roohi Ahmed, the founder and chair of the Gift Wellness Foundation and the Halimah Trust. I first met Zareen at a leadership conference run by the incredible Dr. Sam Collins, CEO of Aspire. (Dr. Sam and her company deserve a mention here, she's a powerhouse in her own right.)

Within minutes of speaking to Zareen, I felt as though we were old friends. Her warmth and authenticity were magnetic, drawing me in with an ease that few people possess. As she began to share her story, I found myself deeply immersed, hanging onto every word.

The raw emotion in her voice made her experiences feel not just heard but profoundly felt. Her deep understanding of her own and others' emotions, coupled with her compassion, radiated so strongly that it felt almost tangible.

In those moments, I knew I was in the presence of someone truly extraordinary. Zareen isn't just a leader; she's a force of nature, connected to a higher purpose that fuels her every action. Her light shines brightly, illuminating a path of inspiration for others to follow.

Zareen's story is a powerful testament to the transformative strength of turning pain into purpose.

From the depths of grief, she has risen as a beacon of hope and an exemplar of soul-led leadership in action. Driven by an unwavering mission and a profound sense of purpose, she is a reminder of just how much one person can achieve when they lead with their soul.

Her journey shows us the immense potential of business as a force for good. Zareen's work is a shining example of how passion and purpose can merge to create meaningful, lasting change in the world.

> **One person can make a difference. You don't have to have a lot of influence. You just have to have faith in your power to change things.**
> **—Norman Vincent Peale**

 **Talking with Zareen**

Three years after the passing of my daughter and having made a solemn promise to her to aid those less fortunate, I established the Halimah School of Excellence in Pakistan. Little did I know this was the beginning of my profound mission.

It all unfolded when I stumbled upon an article in a magazine shedding light on the plight of women in refugee camps who lacked access to menstrual pads, resorting to using shreds of fabric from their clothes. At that moment, a seed was planted within me. A determination to create a social enterprise that would provide these women with dignity through the gift of wellness in the form of menstrual pads.

Embracing Challenges to Reach the Wider World

As I set to work, and while investigating and planning my business model to help others abroad, I found the magnitude of the problem in Britain to be a profound revelation. It was encapsulated in two simple words, period poverty. The undeniable correlation between financial hardship and the struggle many faced in accessing menstrual products.

A struggle affecting girls in schools, homeless women, survivors of abuse, and those relying on the food banks. What caught me off guard was the realisation that a significant portion of those seeking aid from food banks were not without employment, but rather trapped in the cycle of low-wage jobs. This silent struggle, affecting millions across the UK, often goes unnoticed.

Driven by a deep-seated desire to bring about change not only on a global scale but also within the confines of my local community, I embarked on a mission to tackle period poverty head-on. Thus, I initiated efforts to supply pads to schools in my city, alongside fostering open discussions and forums to raise awareness and educate others about the intricacies of menstrual cycles.

In recognizing the critical need for action within my own backyard, I took the first steps towards effecting change, understanding that transformation begins with addressing the challenges closest to home.

Putting the Soul Leader ahead of the Leader

When structure in the business foundation was needed, I found that I had to put a few things in place. It was essential to put the Soul Leader ahead of the leader when seeking to raise funds, as the conversations we have when we reach deep inside us are much more powerful than those driven by our heads.

When you're emotionally connected and aligned with the project's intention and frequency, assistance from others naturally follows. Meaningful interactions with others are the how to make things happen; conversations grounded in recognition of the higher purpose often lead to genuine help.

In every pursuit, it's crucial to infuse the soul so we can connect emotionally to create the desired impact.

If you aim to positively influence others, connecting with them at soul level, and uniting your essence with the purpose behind your actions, is essential. You'll notice that by linking emotions and energy to the ripple effect of your efforts, you can organically expand the reach of what you are pursuing and make a lasting difference.

A Business can be a Vehicle for Compassion and Positive Change in the World

A business can be a vehicle for compassion and positive change. For every pack of menstrual products we sell, we donate pads to women who can't access or afford them. With the help of our period poverty charity, we've donated seven million so far to homeless and refugee women, food banks, schools, and shelters.

The Gift Wellness Foundation is a pledge to leave a positive imprint on the lives of women and our shared environment. It is my pathway to contributing meaningfully to society while upholding the promise I made to my daughter.

> **If your true intentions are to help others, you'll find within you the power you need.**
> **—Mario Alonso Puig**

Period Poverty Statistics around the World

Estimates vary, but research shows period poverty exists in both richer and poorer countries. Every day, millions are likely to be making decisions about whether to buy food or to buy menstrual products, while others simply don't have access to the products and facilities that would let them manage their periods with dignity.

The World Bank estimates at least 500 million women and girls globally lack access to the facilities they need to manage their periods. Meanwhile, 1.25 billion women and girls have no access to a safe, private toilet; 526 million don't have a toilet at all.

Statistics from the UK

In recent years, we've rightly seen in the media a greater focus on period poverty as it affects people in richer countries in the Global North; the UK is no exception.

Indeed, it was estimated that more than 137,700 girls in the UK missed some school last year because they couldn't afford sanitary products. Six per cent of parents said they had been so desperate to equip their daughters with menstrual products that they had resorted to stealing. More than a fifth of parents said they had gone without something themselves so that they had enough money to meet their daughters' needs.

And as in many countries across the world, period poverty in the UK has worsened due to the COVID-19 pandemic. A recent survey by Plan International UK found more than a third of girls ages 14–21 in the UK struggled to afford or access menstrual products during the pandemic—up one-fifth on the previous year. This is equivalent to over one million girls. Half of these girls said they did not have enough money to buy period products at all at some point over the past year, and three-quarters (73 per cent) of those had to use toilet paper as an alternative to period products, like pads.

In the UK, just as in poorer countries, too many girls are being denied their right to fulfil their immense potential and thrive as they grow up.

> **I'm no longer accepting the things I cannot change. I'm changing the things I cannot accept.**
> **—Angela Davis**

Soul-leading story: Channelling Grief as the Fuel to Lead and Do Good in the World

Since primary school, my daughter and I have always been passionate about helping others. When Halimah was thirteen years old, we made a pact that the two of us would establish our own charity and ethical business when she finished university.

At nineteen years old, Halimah secured the course of her dreams at university to study international relations specializing in third-world development. It was six weeks into her course that Halimah was abducted and murdered; ironically, I was working at the time on creating peace and reconciliation to fight against terrorists.

For the first few days after Halimah passed, I was dormant, facing my worst fears, questioning how I was going to survive this and if the pain was going to kill me. I felt I could not just abandon my other child and husband but felt that I could not feel love because it was too painful; I needed to do love.

One day, while lying in bed, I felt my daughter's presence, and right after that, I went through a reawakening phase. I felt fearless as I had been facing my worst fear. All I could think about was that I needed to fulfil the promise I had made to Halimah when she was alive, that of doing the work we both were going to do together.

Within a few weeks, we had established a charity in Halimah's name, and three years later, we had built a school for 434 orphaned and needy girls in Pakistan. The school was named after her, as it was Halimah who initially had the seed of this idea long before she passed. The Halimah School of Excellence was born, and after some time, a college opened next to it. The Halimah campus currently educates and cares for over one thousand girls.

I was on my way back from Pakistan after having inaugurated the Halimah School of Excellence. I was sitting in the lounge at the airport, and all I was thinking about was that I needed to return to work, as I hadn't worked for three years. I knew that whatever I did needed to be in connection with charity.

It was there that I opened a magazine; the page showed an article about this refugee camp and explained how women have to take strips off the bottom of their clothes to fold up into makeshift sanitary pads. It explained how womanhood is used against them like a weapon of war. At that moment, I saw myself giving pads to these women. I saw my innermost purpose shared in that mission.

I got up and raised my hands in the air as if it was happening, to realise seconds later that I was still at the airport lounge. That moment was the birth of a social enterprise, a project born from a profound sense of purpose, enabling the provision of pads to women in dire straits. When thinking about the business model, I decided this would be an enterprise where for every pack I sold, another one would go to helping women in need.

My first container arrived in 2013, and the first thing I did was call the local charity for them to come and collect several pallets. This charity, I heard, was transporting aid to the same refugee camp I had read about in the magazine.

To my surprise, the guy on the phone told me that their container was taking important things like medicines, clothes, and blankets and they would take my things another time. I asked him where he was, and I went to see him. I sat him down and asked him to imagine his mother, sister, and daughter were displaced or in a refugee camp, and no matter what was happening, they were going to get their periods.

I explained how this aid he was taking was for someone's mother, daughter, and sister. In shock, this man took my pallets in his container, recognising that they had been missing such an important part of aid.

After a few years of growing my business like this and supporting others abroad, I learned about period poverty in schools around England and my hometown. Some customers approached me to help, and that was when the Gift Wellness Foundation, a registered charity focused on eliminating period poverty, was born.

Since then, it has been my mission to lead an organisation that not only supports eliminating period poverty, but also changes and shifts how we see our natural cycles. I am here to lead and inject a new way of thinking into how we see periods in every space I can.

It is my intention and hope that this enterprise brings to light the acknowledgement that this apparent weakness in our menstrual cycle is the most miraculous and precious gift in the universe; the gift of being able to give life.

When we lead with our souls, we can do good despite pain and difficulties. For me, it goes full circle, passing on that sacred trust of bringing love to the next generation of leaders, passing on the decision of not just to feel love but to do love.

Advice for Future Leaders

Harness emotional connections for positive influence.

When aspiring to positively impact others, forge genuine connections, and align your soul with the purpose behind your actions. By linking emotions and energy to the why of your actions, you create a ripple effect for others extending far beyond immediate interactions. This approach naturally amplifies the reach of your efforts, promoting organic and lasting change.

Soul-Leading Thought

Don't just feel love, do love.

> **Be the change that you wish to see in the world.**
> —**Arleen Lorrance**

A Creative Experience: Connect with Your Soul's Essence

This exercise invites you to align with and strengthen the core of your being, nurturing both inner peace and self-compassion.

The soul often feels intangible, easily overlooked in our busy lives. This practice will help you bring it into focus, cultivating greater awareness and care for this hidden yet vital dimension of yourself. Regularly tending to your soul not only fortifies your core values but also enhances your connection with others.

Close your eyes and imagine your soul as a secret garden; a private sanctuary within. Take a moment to observe its state. Is it dry, lush, vibrant, or in need of attention? Simply notice without judgment.

Now, step into the role of a gardener. Begin by gently removing anything that feels lifeless or heavy, clearing space for renewal. Prune and tidy until your garden feel ready for new life.

Next, plant seeds or flowers that resonate with your values and deepest desires. What does your dream garden look like? Add elements that bring you joy, perhaps vibrant blossoms, soft moss, or a sparkling fountain. Water the soil with care, imagining this nourishment as your attention and love flowing into your inner self.

When your garden feels complete, pause, and notice the transformation. How does it feel to connect with this enriched inner world?

When you're ready, gently return to the present moment. Carry the renewed sense of self-awareness into your day. As you nurture your inner garden, you may find it easier to extend compassion to others. When applied often, it becomes a natural extension of your own self-care.

Sports: Building unity through leadership

In the world of sports, where competition and camaraderie bring people together, a new era of leadership has emerged, one that stems with the soul. These leaders act as the sturdy pillars that support not only their teams but entire communities. Their influence goes far beyond scores and statistics, transcending strategy, and tactics to reach the deeper realms of empathy, inspiration, and integrity.

Soul-led sports leaders inherently understand their responsibilities extend well beyond the field, court, or pitch. They are not merely strategists; they are guardians of team spirit, architects of culture, and champions of core values. They nurture an environment where individuals can thrive not just as athletes, but as whole human beings.

These leaders have a unique ability to motivate and uplift, igniting a sense of pride, belonging, and shared purpose among their teams and fans alike.

Through their words and actions, they knit narratives of resilience, sportsmanship, and unity that transcend the boundaries of wins and losses. For them, true success isn't measured by trophies or accolades alone; it's reflected in the lives they touch and the hearts they inspire.

In this new era of sportsmanship, victory is as much about the connections forged and the lessons learned along the journey as it is about the final score.

Leading with Soul represents a transformative model of sports leadership, one that focuses the holistic well-being of players. These leaders don't just build strong teams; they cultivate vibrant communities and lasting camaraderie. Their legacy endures, ensuring the spirit of the game thrives for generations to come.

Bruno Saltor: A Soulful Leader in Football

Bruno Saltor is a football coach and former professional player whose career highlights include playing for Espanyol, Almería, and Valencia.

During his remarkable seven-year tenure at Brighton & Hove Albion, he not only excelled as a player but also served as captain, earning the respect of his teammates and fans alike. Following his playing career, Bruno transitioned into leadership roles, starting as a senior player development coach at Brighton before joining Chelsea alongside manager Graham Potter in September 2022.

I first encountered Bruno's story through his interview on the Different Hats podcast. As I listened, I was struck by his humility and the profound influence his parents had on shaping his core values. Bruno spoke with heartfelt sincerity about his childhood dreams of football greatness and the relentless dedication it took to make them a reality. He also shared candid reflections on the highs and lows of his journey, from the exhilarating victories to the darker, more challenging moments.

By the end of the podcast, I was convinced that Bruno's insights belonged in this book.

When I had the opportunity to interview him, our conversation went even deeper into the impact of leading others in sports. Bruno spoke with remarkable openness about the foundational role of values, the power of consistency, and the transformative impact of unity and self-reflection in shaping our paths as leaders.

Bruno Saltor doesn't just embody these principles; he lives them. His approach to guiding and coaching others demonstrates what it means to guide with heart and integrity in the world of professional sports. His story serves as an inspiring testimony to the power of Leading with Soul in sports. A reminder that leadership transcends the game, rooted instead in the nurturing of the human spirit.

 **Talking with Bruno**

When I think about how I coach or lead others, I often overlook my strengths until others point them out. It was people around me, my peers, colleagues, and wife who recognised qualities in me that they saw as leadership. I never claimed that title for myself; I was just being true to who I am. It's consistency, discipline, self-reflection, and care for others that they saw in me, qualities that pave the way for long-term success, not short-term gains.

Building Confidence

Leadership skills are something we can develop and learn over time. One of the best ways to learn leadership is by observing other leaders in action. The more you watch, the more you can absorb and integrate those skills into your approach. It's not just about imitating others; it's about combining those skills with strong self-awareness and values.

When you merge progress with a deep understanding of who you are and what you stand for, you become the influence you admire in others.

Nowadays, we're fortunate to have an abundance of leadership examples to draw inspiration from. Whether it's the consistent performers, the charismatic speakers, or the soulful leaders who focus on harmony and balance within their teams, there's a style for everyone to aspire to.

As I embarked on my leadership journey, I took the time to reflect on what kind of leader I wanted to be. I considered my unique skills and how I could leverage them to serve others.

I've always been inspired by leaders who aren't afraid to think outside the box. Philip Douglas Jackson, for example, is an American former professional basketball player, coach, and executive. He is someone I admire and a great example of someone who lead with his soul. Jackson is known as the Zen Master. Jackson's approach to coaching basketball transcended the game itself. His unconventional methods, like the pregame ritual of holding hands with his entire team, or sharing books among players, inspired me. I've gained invaluable leadership insights from him, incorporating some of his philosophy into my coaching style.

And it's not just Jackson; leaders like Simon Sinek and many others inspire me with their empathy and authenticity. What sets these leaders apart isn't their job titles or accolades; it's their genuine care for others and how they make people feel that makes them unique. That's the hallmark of true leadership, people are naturally drawn to those who are themselves and genuinely care.

Ultimately, leadership isn't just about leading; it's about the positive impact those guiding others have on those around them.

A Human centred approach to Leadership

We can all be part of a new way to lead. We're witnessing a shift in how leadership is perceived and practised, and each of us has a role in this transformation.

At home, parents play a central role in nurturing the leaders of tomorrow. While schools must contribute, the responsibility cannot rest solely on their shoulders.

Leadership comes in many forms and it's deeply personal. What resonates as effective leadership for one person may differ for another. Our society may not yet be ready to embrace teaching leadership as a formal subject in schools. However, there's much we can do to introduce these values and ways of being early on. As parents and coaches, it's our responsibility to reform the process, accelerating the arrival of that moment.

In the past, we lacked the knowledge and self-awareness to fully understand certain aspects of human nature, and thus couldn't address what we couldn't perceive. Today, we're embracing a new model, a newfound openness to different ways of being. We mustn't compare the past with the present; instead, let's focus on the progress we're making towards a more dynamic future.

Leadership is evolving towards a more humanistic approach, and we can serve as facilitators for this change. In football, for example, we're changing how we communicate with players, promoting environments where individuals feel safe discussing their challenges and adversities. Although we are continuously embracing new ways of coaching and leading, we must bear in mind that change of any kind doesn't happen overnight; it requires steady consistency.

Creating Safe Environments

There's been a noticeable emergence of a new breed of coaches and leaders armed with knowledge previously out of reach for many. With a deeper grasp of human psychology and behaviours, we're better prepared to drive meaningful change.

For instance, consider the creation of safe spaces for players. Our focus is on establishing environments where players feel comfortable expressing themselves without fear of backlash. It's about crafting spaces that players willingly want to be part of, knowing they'll be seen, heard, and valued.

When players feel safe, they're more likely to speak up and be their authentic selves. Establishing this sense of safety is just the beginning; our next step is to closely understand each player and their unique abilities, tailoring our approach to nurture their talents. This approach fosters the growth and development of players.

Mindset plays an important role in my coaching philosophy. By prioritising mindset, we're able to block out external distractions and focus on our goals. The focus is on taking intentional steps, one at a time, while blocking out the noise of external influences. We concentrate solely on the question, "What's next?" and then take action accordingly. Ultimately, while we can't control external factors, there's immense power in harnessing our internal focus and drive.

Using All Your Resources When Making Decisions

Sports are a competitive field, so it's essential to think about your approach and goals before engaging in any competitive activity. Some place all their attention into maintaining a balance between sports and other areas of their lives, while others are willing to devote most of their time to sports, almost becoming an obsession. Knowing what you want to achieve in sports can help prevent disappointment and unmet expectations.

In life, every decision has a cost. Many people, especially young people, aren't aware that successful individuals have paid a significant price to achieve their goals. When making decisions, consider not just one but multiple resources, such as skills, intuition, personal values, and the question of whether you'll be able to sleep soundly after making your choice. Determine if the cost of your decision is worth it for you, your family, and your time.

Wishing Isn't Enough

Coaches' and leaders' jobs are to help young people focus on the present moment. Many young people believe they have ample time to achieve their goals and dream big without considering the necessary steps to reach them. Unfortunately, not everyone accomplishes their aspirations. Although having potential is great, fulfilling your dreams requires more than just wishing. It needs altering your habits and behaviours to align with your vision, which requires hard work, consistency, and discipline. It can be challenging to stay engaged and focused, especially for a seventeen-year-old brimming with energy.

Navigating Challenges with Agility

As a football player, you're often immersed in the present moment, embodying your authentic self on the field. However, transitioning into a coaching or leadership role demands a different skill set. It's no longer about me, but about adopting a sense of unity and teamwork; it's about we.

Evolving from player to leader requires deep reflection on your decisions as you become the essential oil that keeps the team machinery running smoothly.

My journey as a football player has been punctuated by challenges, each offering invaluable lessons on leadership. These experiences have crystallized my vision of the type of leader I aspire to be. Walking in the shoes of my players and understanding their struggles and pain points has been instrumental in shaping my approach. It's often said that a healed individual is more radiant than one who has never faced adversity.

I'm committed to continuous growth and self-development. Prioritizing empathy, kindness, and honesty allows me to be the best version of myself, knowing that my actions have ripple effects on others.

My intention is not solely to guide but to serve and evolve alongside my team, steering us in the same direction of growth and progress. After all, leadership isn't just about authority; it's about collective growth and fulfilment.

Working on Being Humble by Putting a Mirror in Front of You Every Time You Win

Embracing humility is fundamental in guiding others towards richer experiences. When we allow our egos to dominate, our growth stagnates. Even in victory, staying humble is the key to continuous evolution.

Balancing a hunger for success with humility is possible by taking a reflective approach to winning. How you react when winning matters.

Hold up a mirror to yourself and observe your reactions when you win. How you handle victory speaks volumes. So, when you achieve success, take a moment to reflect. Acknowledge your triumphs and what you've done well; then consider areas for improvement. This introspective process fuels ongoing growth.

When losing, keep in mind that while perfection may be elusive, inner peace is attainable through daily reflection. Ask yourself if you've given your best effort each day. Have you adequately prepared? Even if mistakes are made or setbacks occur, find solace in knowing you've done your utmost. Many external factors are not within our control, but we can be at peace. Learn from the experience, prepare for the next challenge, and move forward with newfound wisdom.

Cultivating Faith in Your Journey

AI is a valuable supporting tool, not a human replacement. It can amplify the game for leaders and coaches. It can help us with accurate information and charts, but you see, it's not just about having this endless knowledge at our fingertips, it's about how we use it and interpret what makes the difference. We've got to be objective, not just subjective.

Remember, we're not playing against machines here; it's humans all the way. And to win, we've got to understand who we're playing with, in this case, humans full of emotions, dramas, sleepless nights, and challenges. Therefore, until we play against machines, we must think like humans, act like humans, and be humans.

Take football, for example. We've got players from all corners of the globe, each with their unique needs, cultures, and backgrounds. We must respect and embrace their emotions and differences. When we do that and when all members of the team understand that it's like unlocking a whole new level of teamwork.

Communication is key in bringing the team together in the same direction. When the team is on the same level, everyone feels valued and validated, together charging towards that same goal. It's not just about playing the game; it's about playing it together, united in our diversity.

AI can be a valuable support tool, not a human replacement, and we must cultivate faith in our journey. Our role as coaches and leaders is to cement everything together and find a balance that benefits everyone.

Finding Unity and Human Connection

Human connection is vital for our well-being. We thrive on it. In today's world, where social media and other distractions often pull us apart, we must come together as a team and set boundaries on what isolates us from one another, replacing it with unity and human connection.

Leaders play a crucial role here, guiding those in their care towards unity and better decision making. For that to happen, we need to truly understand what it means to be human and get in touch with the essence of who we are. So, we can create cultures with strong identities that embrace ways of being and behaving that align with who we are as human beings.

It's true; not everyone is ready for this journey at the same time. But by creating safe environments where everyone feels seen and heard, we can accelerate the readiness of those who may not be ready.

Pausing to Hear

And then there's the power of the pause. Pausing is of great help to take stock of our challenges as individuals and as a collective. When we pause, we can reflect and explore what needs to happen and how we can serve best.

Marcus Aurelius hit the nail on the head when he said, "All our problems come from our inability to pause." Our job is not to force people to pause but to empower them to take moments of introspection. These deliberate pauses allow individuals to emerge fortified with clarity and resilience, ready to tackle whatever comes their way.

Let's take a collective breath, acknowledge our challenges, explore our human essence, and ask how we can serve each other best. Together, connected and in unity, we can navigate the challenges of an ever-evolving world.

Values as the Staples of Life

Values are fundamental pillars of our existence, shaping our essence and defining our identity as we interact with the world. They transcend mere words, evolving into powerful expressions of our beliefs conveyed through actions that resonate louder than any speech. Our daily actions and choices serve as reflections of what holds the utmost significance to us.

When we lead with authenticity, anchoring ourselves in our values becomes paramount. They serve as our guiding compass, navigating us through the intricate terrain of decision making and providing a moral framework for our conduct.

Leading from the heart necessitates a spirit of selflessness, prioritizing the needs of others and the common good above personal interests. At times, it demands making sacrifices for the collective and the greater system, driven by the conviction that it's the right course of action. Strong values serve as the bedrock for making such decisions, offering stability in the world of soulful leadership.

My upbringing laid the groundwork for me, instilling values of respect and inclusivity that extend beyond mere education. It highlighted the importance of understanding oneself and empathizing with others, recognizing the influence of backgrounds on behaviours and perspectives. When I mentor others, I carry these lessons with me.

Growing up in an environment that nurtured deep self-awareness and respect has profoundly influenced my approach to life, leadership, and coaching. Living out these values and staying attuned to my essence have become second nature, a testament to the nurturing environment I was fortunate to have. My inner self, my soul, seamlessly embodies these values; it's not a conscious effort but rather an intrinsic part of who I am, guiding my every action. I owe much of this to the values instilled in me during my formative years and the guidance of my parents.

In leadership roles, you have to understand that you will have to take smart risks that will make you feel uncomfortable. Whether the decision directly impacts you or not, if it benefits the collective, it's the correct course of action. Placing the well-being of others above personal desires is key for good leadership. When decisions are made with this mindset, there's assurance in knowing the right thing was done.

I often find myself revisiting this question: "Will I be able to sleep well tonight with this decision, or will regret keep me tossing and turning?" Is this decision in the best interest of my team and my family?" It's not just a passing thought; it serves as a guiding principle for ethical decision making.

Certainly, we all aim for contentment before bedtime, but tough decisions can make that difficult. It's not about being pleased with every outcome; it's about resting peacefully, knowing integrity guided the choice.

At our core, all humans seek the same fundamental desires: safety, belonging, significance, and purpose. When these elements meet, peace follows.

We have an innate ability to discern authenticity. Remember, perfection isn't necessary; authenticity is. Stay true to yourself, prioritising your values and what holds meaning for you, as being genuine and compassionate brings lasting fulfilment. Regardless of the outcomes, peace will be yours to embrace.

Soul-Leading Story: Navigate Discomfort and Uncertainty with Resilience and Grace

In one of my toughest years as a professional player, I faced numerous challenges. I battled injuries and struggled to maintain my usual level of performance. External pressures loomed larger than ever, pushing me into a downward spiral of emotional closure. Instead of seeking help and solutions, I focused outside myself, losing sight of my voice in the process. I was pointing outward rather than inward.

Emotionally drained and feeling disconnected, I knew something had to change. So, I decided to change my environment, ultimately transforming my life. This new space allowed me to reflect on my actions and mindset, leading to a crucial change of mind. I needed to take ownership of my journey and point the finger inwards.

By turning my focus inwards, I discovered the power of self-honesty, pausing, and self-reflection. I explored how I could have approached things differently. I learned that I have to be true to myself in any context or environment. My focus and attention needed to change, as I wouldn't always have the opportunity to change the environment to take a breath.

Leading with Soul

In embracing my authentic self, I learned to navigate discomfort and uncertainty with resilience and grace. These invaluable lessons became the basis of my personal and professional growth and development.

Now armed with a deeper understanding of myself and in touch with my essence again, I use these insights to guide and support others on their paths.

As a coach, I emphasize the importance of mindset, teaching my players to focus inwards and seek solutions amidst life's challenges. By doing so, we can quiet the noise in our heads and pave the way for growth and development.

Overcoming these challenges equipped me to acknowledge the layers of emotions that, at times, we can't fully understand. I can now pass on to my players how self-awareness, self-reflection, and focusing inwards to overcome challenges are essential for personal and professional growth. This is the value of self-honesty, vulnerability, and accepting one's emotions.

Through my journey, I've become a better listener and leader, recognizing the struggles of my players and others with a newfound perspective. I've learned that the only competition worth engaging in is with ourselves. By competing against ourselves and striving to be the best version of who we can be, we become better equipped to support others on their journeys.

In the end, it's not about what happens on the field but about looking inwards for personal growth and self-discovery, which can profoundly impact both physical performance and personal life.

The key to improvement lies within ourselves. With that in mind, I continue to dedicate myself to consistent self-improvement, knowing that being true to who I am and leading with my soul are the foundation of how I choose to live. Now it's time to walk the talk.

Advice to Future Leaders

- Be yourself in a way that is kind, humble, and honest.
- Focus on what you want to create for your team and the world, and make decisions based on that, not on how it looks outside or what the world is telling you.
- In every action you take, consider kindness and honesty.
- Nobody ever regrets being themselves.
- Consistently ask, "How can I best serve today?"
- Everyone in your place of work is of value; every role matters and understanding the needs of the people you lead influences your collective achievements.

Soul-Leading Thoughts

- When challenges come, lean forward, viewing them as opportunities for growth.
- Effective leaders prepare successors for continuity and progress.
- True leadership requires selflessly dedicating yourself to collective success.
- We can't control what happens to us, only how we respond.
- Look inwards for contentment while recognizing the ongoing journey of learning.
- Genuine leadership naturally inspires and guides others towards positive action.
- The impact you leave on others is determined by how you make them feel.
- True leaders compete with themselves, not others.
- Focusing on self-improvement creates an ethos of excellence in those around you.

A healed human being is much more beautiful than a human being who never suffered.

—Bruno Saltor, Sports Leader, Football Coach, and Former Player

A Creative Experience: Aligning Your Body Towards Deeper Self-Awareness

This exercise is designed to help you cultivate a deeper awareness of your body, encouraging both self-understanding and a greater sensitivity to others. By taking time to connect with your physical self, you pave the way for emotional alignment. Let's begin.

Scan Your Body

Find a quiet, comfortable place to sit or lie down. Close your eyes if it feels natural and start by scanning your body from head to toe. Notice areas of discomfort or tension. Simply acknowledge them without judgment or the need to "fix" them. Turn your attention to the parts of your body that feel good. Offer gratitude to these areas for their quiet and consistent support, even when unnoticed. Take a few deep breaths as you settle into this awareness.

Cherish Your Body

Imagine your body as something you treasure deeply. Perhaps it's: A cherished book filled with wisdom. A luxurious car you care for meticulously. A beloved friend who has always been there for you. Choose something that feels meaningful to you; something you would handle with care, attention, and love.

Embody That Care

Now, shift your focus back to your body: Picture how your body might feel as this treasured object. Is it smooth, sturdy, delicate, or solid? Imagine lavishing your body with the same care you'd extend to something you deeply cherish. Perhaps you envision: Gently caressing it with tenderness. Whispering words of appreciation. Giving it the focused attention, it deserves. Ask yourself: What does my body need right now? Is it rest, hydration, movement, or simply acknowledgment? Allow yourself to meet this need with genuine care.

Reflect on the Experience

Stay with this awareness for a few moments. As you do, notice any sensations or emotions that arise. How does it feel to treat yourself with such kindness? Has this exercise shifted how you perceive your body or yourself?

Transition and Commit

When you feel ready, gently bring your awareness back to your surroundings. Reflect on how you feel in this moment. Ask yourself: Is there one small action I can take to enhance my physical well-being today? Maybe you'll adjust your posture, take a stretch break, drink some water, or simply take a deep breath. Commit to honouring your body's needs throughout the day.

Daily Practice and Celebration

Make this a daily ritual, even if only for a few minutes. Over time, observe how these moments of care impact your body and your overall sense of self-awareness. Celebrate the subtle changes, whether it's feeling more at ease, finding greater relaxation, or cultivating a stronger bond with yourself.

Remember, every small act of self-care is a powerful step toward deeper alignment with yourself. It's not about perfection but about consistent, mindful actions that lead to profound transformation. Honour your body as the incredible vessel it is. It deserves nothing less.

Home: Where Everything Begins

Some of the most inspiring leaders never make the headlines. They don't stand in the spotlight or magazine covers, but their impact is no less remarkable.

They're leaders who work quietly and diligently behind the scenes, shaping the world in unique ways. They're children, moms and dads who run their households with love and care, and teachers who motivate their students to reach new heights. They are people who overcome illnesses and use their traumas as healing tools for others. They are mentors who guide others on the path to recovery.

Their stories may not be glitzy, but they are powerful and impactful. It's astonishing how much of a difference they can make without ever asking for recognition.

Jacob's Pieces of Wisdom

A few years ago, while I was conversing with my twelve-year-old son, he shared an incident that left me thinking long after our conversation ended. He told me about an encounter with an elderly person who had spoken down to him, assuming authority simply based on age. As a parent, my instinct was to teach him what I was taught as a child: to respect his elders no matter what and take it on the chin. His response caught me off guard.

In a calm and composed manner, he expressed his disagreement, challenging the notion that respect should be automatically granted based on hierarchy or age alone.

Jacob spoke of respect as something earned through understanding, empathy, and compassion and said that, in any case, should he take advantage of his position as a child, it was for the older person to make him feel safe, inviting engagement. A concept far more profound than I had anticipated from a twelve-year-old. From that moment, my son became my unexpected teacher, and I was an eager student.

His words prompted a shift in my perception of family and societal structures. I realised that the way we perceive structures, traditions, and norms must evolve to accommodate the insights and perspectives of new generations.

At just twelve years old, Jacob embodied a leadership style characterized by his own and other's awareness, respect, and inclusivity; qualities of someone leading with his soul. His ability to engage with others, based not on hierarchical power dynamics but on genuine care and respect, was a revelation for me.

My son taught me a valuable lesson: age does not define wisdom, and leadership transcends mere authority or place in the structure.

True leadership, as he demonstrated, lies in creating an environment where every person feels safe to speak, is seen, and is heard, regardless of age or stature.

From that day forward, I vowed to approach family dynamics with newfound perception, changing the structure in which we operated at home so our children would feel respected, heard, and seen, not just for being children but for being part of the team.

In the end, what taught me this lesson wasn't my years of experience but the fresh perspective of a child who dared to challenge conventional structure and wisdom.

And for that, I am forever grateful.

> **Anything unrecognized becomes uncelebrated. Anything uncelebrated becomes unrewarded. Anything unrewarded eventually exits your life. In short, whatever you recognize increases in value, and whatever you don't recognize decreases in value.**
> **—Dr Mike Murdock**

John and Sarah's Story

Consider the story of my clients, the Anderson family. John and Sarah Anderson, parents to three children, found themselves facing a challenging situation when their youngest, Emma, was diagnosed with a learning disability. Instead of viewing it as an obstacle, the Andersons embraced the opportunity to become Soul Leaders within their family.

John and Sarah recognised that Emma's growth and well-being were intertwined with the overall flourishing of their family. They approached Emma's challenges with a desire for her personal development as well as a broader vision of creating an environment where each family member could learn and thrive.

John and Sarah led with both heart and mind. They sought to understand Emma's unique needs and strengths and create an atmosphere of unconditional love and support within their home.

Their approach wasn't just about addressing Emma's learning disability; it was about cultivating an environment where every member felt valued, heard, and encouraged to pursue their passions.

The Andersons became supporters for inclusive education, working with Emma's school to create a supportive learning environment.

They engaged in open communication with their other children, which encouraged openness and understanding. The family began participating in community events related to learning disabilities and created a network of support not only for Emma but for others facing similar challenges.

John and Sarah's journey demonstrate the transformative impact of leading with both heart and mind. By focusing on everyone's growth, they created a positive ripple effect that extended beyond their home and into their community.

> **What we know matters, but who we are matters more.**
>
> —Brené Brown

METAPHOR FOR LEADERS

A Metaphor for Soul-Led Leadership: Swimming to Japan

Written by Sue Knight in NLP at Work, this story beautifully captures the essence of adaptability, resilience, and having clarity in where we are going:

Once upon a time, there was a couple who had achieved many of their ambitions in life, yet there was one main goal outstanding: they wanted to swim to Japan.

They reflected on this goal for a long time, and one day they set off. They were not used to swimming, so they found it difficult. They were acutely aware of how heavy their limbs felt. They ached with the constant effort, especially when the strong current was against them. Gradually, however, their bodies got used to swimming, and they developed a style that was effortless and rhythmical.

They noticed the water around them—how it changed colour as the days went by. In the early morning, it would be clear and blue, and in certain lights, it sparkled emerald green. As the sun set, it developed the rich warm colours of the evening sky.

They also became aware of the creatures in the water—the small silver fish that swam with them during the day, and the dark shadows that skimmed by them in the deep. They noticed how the sound of the waves changed as the water lapped their ears. They could feel the subtle changes of the weather as breezes turned into winds and then died down again.

They learned how to find food in the water, how to nourish themselves, and how to use their bodies effortlessly. Over time, they developed a refined sense of smell, allowing them to detect changes in the environment by the scent carried to them on the breeze.

They swam for days and weeks with no sight of land. Then, one day, they saw the dark profile of land on the horizon. They swam on and recognized the shoreline of Japan. As they approached, they became quiet and eventually looked at each other. In that moment, they knew.

Without hesitation, they turned back to the sea and swam on.

This metaphor reveals the essence of soul-led leadership.

Ask yourself these questions to relate with the teachings from the story:

- How did the couple's approach change over time?
- What did they do differently that allowed them to persevere?
- What tools, skills, or mindsets did they develop to achieve their goal?
- How can you apply their approach to your own leadership journey?

Think about how modelling skills like: Awareness, resilience, adaptability, clarity, and focus can bring you closer to your goals.

A Creative Experience: for a Well-Defined Vision

Clarity and focus are essential for impactful decisions and progress. This exercise will help you articulate a clear, actionable vision and align it with your core values.

Define Your Vision

Think of a goal, outcome, or transformation you want for yourself or your team. Be specific and state it in positive language. For instance, instead of "I want to be less stressed," try "I will practice daily mindfulness to feel calm and focused."

Explore the Why

- Why is this vision important to me?
- How does it align with my values and beliefs?
- What will achieving it mean for me and those I lead?

Bring It to Life, Visualize the result.

- What will you see, hear, and feel when it becomes reality?
- How will you know you've achieved it?

Assess the Impact, how this vision will affect others.

- Who benefits from this outcome?
- What ripple effects might it create for your community, team, or family?

Take Small, Steady Actions

Identify one small step you can take today to move closer to your vision. Then, commit to repeating or refining this step daily. Small shifts lead to big transformations.

Revisit your vision and its steps often, refining as needed, and stay flexible as challenges arise.

Remember, clear direction is the compass of soul-led leadership, and this practice keeps you aligned with your vision and goals.

Check Lists to Assess Your Current Leadership Style

This questionnaire aims to prompt leaders like you to reflect deeply on your values, reasons, and approach to your why, what, where, and who so you lead and live a life characterized by empathy, integrity, and commitment.

1. **Self-Reflection**
    a. How would you describe your leadership style?
    b. What values guide your decisions?
    c. Think about a recent decision you made as a leader. Did it align with your personal values and purpose?

2. **Purpose and Vision**
    a. What is your personal purpose as a leader?
    b. How does your purpose align with the vision of your organisation, household, or team?
    c. How do you communicate your ideas and vision in a way that inspires others?

3. **Authenticity and Integrity**
    a. How do you ensure authenticity in the way you lead?
    b. What steps do you take to maintain integrity in your interactions and decisions?

c. Describe a time when you faced a challenge to your integrity as a leader and how you handled it.
   d. Think of the why that drives your choices. Uncovering why you are making each choice brings you closer to what is important to you.

4. **Empathy and Compassion**
   a. How do you cultivate empathy within your people?
   b. Share an example of how you've demonstrated compassion towards others during difficult times.
   c. How do you balance empathy and accountability when you lead?

5. **Servant Leadership**
   a. How do you put at the centre of you attention the needs of the people you lead?
   b. Describe a situation where you acted as a servant leader to empower others.
   c. In what ways do you encourage collaboration and collective growth within your team, household, or organisation?

6. **Mindfulness and Self-Care**
   a. How do you prioritise self-care and well-being as a leader?

b. What practices do you engage in to maintain mindfulness and mental clarity?
   c. How do you promote a culture of well-being and work-life balance within your team, household, or organisation?

7. **Continuous Learning and Growth**
   a. How do you approach personal and professional development as a leader?
   b. Share a recent learning experience that has influenced your leadership philosophy.
   c. How do you encourage a culture of learning and growth among your team members?
   d. How do you deal with conflict? Are you an eager fighter, or can you find a way through tense emotions to higher ground? Think of a specific scenario that you experienced and what you learned from it.

8. **Impact and Legacy**
   a. What legacy do you hope to leave as a leader?
   b. How do you measure the impact of your leadership beyond tangible results?
   c. Describe a meaningful interaction or transformational moment you've experienced as a leader.

Now that you have some answers, think of new ways to lead that honour your responses and the essence of who you are.

> **I keep six honest serving men. (They taught me all I knew.) Their names are What and Why and When and How and Where and Who.**
>
> **—Rudyard Kipling**

Humanity's moment in an AI World

As the world rapidly transforms under the influence of AI, we stand at a crossroads. This isn't just a moment of technological advancement; it's a defining moment for humanity that calls for us to lead with courage, compassion, and clarity.

The question isn't whether AI will change our lives; it already has. The question is: how will we respond?

Will we allow ourselves to be swept along, losing sight of what makes us human? Or will we rise to the challenge, embracing the wisdom of our souls and leading with integrity, empathy, and courage?

The answer lies within us.

This book isn't just about leadership in the traditional sense. It's about showing up for yourself, your family, community, and the world. It's about recognising that the greatest leaders aren't those who control the most resources or influence the largest audiences. The greatest leaders are those who connect deeply, honestly, and with purpose.

As you move forward, I encourage you to ask yourself:

> What does it mean for me to lead with soul?
>
> How can I balance the opportunities of AI with the irreplaceable qualities of humanity?
>
> How can I nurture deeper relations in my life and work?

Leadership begins within. When we are authentic, when we honour our values, embrace our humanity, and live with intention, we inspire others to do the same.

You hold the key to shaping a more human, soul-led future. The steps you take today will echo through the lives you touch. Let this book be your companion as you take that journey.

The world needs leaders who are willing to be vulnerable, who care, and create spaces where humanity thrives. You can be that leader. You have the power to make a difference.

This is humanity's moment. Let's seize it together.

There will be people in this life who will cut you open just to see what you are made of ... show them it is love.
—Donna Ashworth

Final Thoughts

As I finished the last chapter of this book, I found myself drawn into a quiet moment of reflection. I closed my eyes, and in the stillness of my mind, an image emerged: a magnificent olive tree.

This tree was unlike any I had ever encountered. Towering and timeless, its gnarled trunk and sweeping branches seemed to whisper ancient wisdom. Its roots, deep and steadfast, anchored it firmly into the earth, unapologetically claiming its rightful space. Above, its canopy stretched wide, offering shade, comfort, and protection. It wasn't just a tree; it was a symbol.

I approached this living giant in my mind's eye, captivated by its abundance. Every branch was heavy with olives, small treasures shimmering with vitality. In its presence, I felt an undeniable sense of being accompanied.

It was as though this tree, silent and serene, held answers to questions I hadn't yet asked.

The peace I felt in that moment was profound, like a soft, warm light wrapping around me. The tree seemed to remind me that amidst the chaos of life, there is always a stillness we can return to. A place where we can root ourselves, renew our energy, and thrive.

When I came out of this meditation, I was curious. What was this tree trying to tell me? Its image lingered in my heart, urging me to understand its message. So, I turned to the wisdom of the world around me and discovered that olive trees have long symbolized connection, renewal, and rebirth. These three words resonated deeply with me because they are the essence of everything, I've wanted to share with you in this book.

A few days later, as if the universe wanted to emphasize the message, I walked into the Florence Davoult Gallery in Bruniquel, France. There, a sculpture of another grand tree greeted me. It was fictional yet brimming with symbolism. Its twisted branches reached out like open arms; its roots carved with intricate detail. A compass was etched into its trunk, and an elephant stood quietly beneath it.

This tree told its own story: stay rooted, know your direction, and never lose touch with your essence. It made me smile. The world is so beautifully aligned when we open ourselves to its messages.

As I reflect on the journey we've taken together in these pages, I see the olive tree as a metaphor for soul-led leadership. It reminds us to stay grounded in our humanity, to connect deeply with others, and to embrace the opportunities for renewal that life offers.

Leadership is more than results or accolades; it's the legacy we leave in the hearts of those we touch. Like the olive tree, may you bring shade and nourishment to those around you. May your roots go deep, your branches stretch wide, and your fruits be abundant.

May your journey of leading with soul be as enriching and timeless as the wisdom of the olive tree.

With warmth and gratitude,
Marina

Acknowledgements

Thank you, Maria Coronado, for your fresh insights and curious questions. A valuable lesson I learned from working with you is that when I think with my head, I tend to overcomplicate things. When you asked me, "Marina, what do you really want to say here?" and I answered from the heart, what I wrote was shorter, simpler, and far more powerful than anything I'd come up with by overthinking. It's funny, I'm always telling others to "keep it simple," yet I needed that gentle reminder myself.

Thank you, Hannah Davies, and my Wales 'boyo' Anna Morgan for loving me with no changes needed.

Thank you to all the leaders, visionaries, and readers who inspired this work: Dominic Mott, Francesca Hamptons, Omar Meza, Sam Thomas, Dr Zareen Roohi Ahmed, and Bruno Saltor. It was an honour to interview you. Thank you for sharing a part of your soul with me. Your words ring daily in my ears.

Thank you, my special readers, for taking your valuable time to read the book: Julie Parkin, Jane Jones, Steve Ball, Nina Butler, and Sue Knight. Your courage to lead authentically and with humanity is what makes this book possible.

Finally, thank you to Carmen, Jacob, and George, my cosmos, and my entire universe.

References

Websites

https://nlpcoach.in/nlp-well-defined-outcomes
www.forbes.com/sites/celinnedacosta/2020/09/29/conscious-leadership-why-its-more-important-than-ever/?sh=7f34a751ecc1
www.forbes.com/sites/richardosibanjo/2021/03/30/the-7-languages-great-leaders-speak
https://en.wikipedia.org/wiki/Phil_Jackson
https://youtu.be/X4Qm9cGRub0?feature=shared
www.aspireforequality.co.uk Dr Sam Collins
https://hbr.org/2011/06/the-happiness-dividend
www.youtube.com/watch?v=viJNOUy3hU8
www.actionaid.org.uk/blog/2022/05/18/period-poverty-statistics-around-world
https://periodpoverty.uk
https://corvirtus.com/blog/becoming-an-authentic-leader-arriving-at-your-destination
Florence Davoult, (tree picture)
www.davoult-florence.book.fr

Podcasts

Different Hats (www.youtube.com/@different-hats)
The Search for the Soulful Leader (www.soulfulleadership.uk)

Books

NLP at Work (second, third, and fourth editions) by Sue Knight
NLP and Leadership by Sue Knight
The Gift by Dr Zareen Roohi Ahmed
Solve for Happy by Mo Gawdat
Scary Smart by Mo Gawdat
Boundaries for Leaders: Results, Relationships, and Being Ridiculously in Charge by Henry Cloud
Start with Why by Simon Sinek
Leaders Eat Last by Simon Sinek
Leader by Katy Granville-Chapman and Emmie Bidston
The Five Dysfunctions of a Team by Patrick Lencioni
Everyday NLP by Florence Madden & Eleni Sarantinou
The Last Season: A Team in Search of Its Soul by Phil Jackson
Daring Greatly by Brené Brown
Be More Unicorn by Joanna Gray

About the Author

Marina Fernández Julian, founder of Marina Zest for Life Coaching and Training, facilitates growth and enables individuals to master self-management and align with their authentic selves. With unwavering dedication, Marina champions the transformative journey towards inner and outer congruence, personal equilibrium, and joyful living.

A dynamic coach and NLP facilitator and trainer, and a fervent life advocate, Marina ardently believes that self-awareness is the cornerstone of crafting an enriching life. Her latest publication, *Balance: Living a Life True to Yourself*, stands as a testament to her depth of understanding and her passion for guiding others towards fulfilment and authenticity.

Marina finds inspiration in sunlit spaces, dancing, culinary delights, and the allure of beauty. A native of Spain who has called England home for over twenty-six years, Marina treasures her roots while embracing the diversity of her experiences. Above all, Marina's heart belongs to her cherished circle of family and friends, for whom she holds the deepest affection.

Whether you are an individual looking for personal coaching, a leader exploring new approaches to leadership, or a company seeking solutions, Marina can help you thrive.

Contact:
Email: marinazestforlife@gmail.com
Website: marinazestforlife.com
Instagram: @marinazestforlife
LinkedIn: Marina Fernández Julian

www.ingramcontent.com/pod-product-compliance
Ingram Content Group UK Ltd.
Pitfield, Milton Keynes, MK11 3LW, UK
UKHW042223151224
452529UK00001B/2